Dear God, HE'S HOME!

A Woman's Guide to Her Stay-at-Home Man

JANET THOMPSON

NEW HOPE
PUBLISHERS
Gospel-Centered. Missions-Driven.

BIRMINGHAM, ALABAMA

New Hope® Publishers
P. O. Box 12065
Birmingham, AL 35202-2065
NewHopeDigital.com
New Hope Publishers is a division of WMU®.

Library of Congress Cataloging-in-Publication Data
Thompson, Janet, 1947-
    Dear God, he's home! : a woman's guide to her stay-at-home man / Janet Thompson.
    pages cm
Includes bibliographical references.
ISBN 978-1-59669-364-7 (sc)
1. Wives--Religious life. 2. Christian women--Religious life. 3. Unemployed--Religious life. 4. Marriage--Religious aspects--Christianity. 5. Househusbands. 6. Unemployment--Psychological aspects. I. Title.
    BV4528.15.T57 2013
    248.8'435--dc23
                                            2012042724

Cover Image: Patrizia Tilly/shutterstock.com
Cover Design: Kay Chin Bishop
Interior Design: Glynese Northam

ISBN-10: 1-59669-364-9
ISBN-13: 978-1-59669-364-7

N134107 • 0313 • 3M1

CONTENTS

DEDICATION

To
Dave, my stay-at-home man and cherished hubby.
Your love and devotion never fail to amaze me.
I love you dearly!
Your wiffy

ACKNOWLEDGMENTS

WITHOUT MY STAY-AT-HOME MAN GRANTING me literary permission to write candidly about our life together, this book could never have emerged from my heart to yours.

Some have said life with me is like an open book. I consider it allowing God to use our real life experiences to help others—mentoring, my passion and my mission. God gets all the glory, not us.

I thank God in all His glory for the blessings of friends, family, and publishers who graciously participate with me in "open-book" life and ministry:

MY HUBBY, DAVE, THE HERO of this book—or as he good-humoredly says, "The sacrificial lamb." You selflessly allow me to write and speak vulnerably and honestly about our messes and our miracles. I love you more with each passing moment—and they are passing quickly these days.

My family inadvertently shares "our story" and indulgingly allows me to tell it all. You are my legacy and my love.

Sharron Pankhurst, my Southern California walking buddy and trusted friend. You always ask with each new book, "Am I going to get to help edit this one?" What a gift to me and to my editors.

Anita Sherwood, my southern Idaho walking buddy, neighbor, and dear friend. You're a gift from God to these two California transplants.

All the brave wives sharing your stories honestly and transparently to encourage, enlighten, and mentor other wives; and stay-at-home man Joseph, for providing a male perspective. I couldn't have written a book to reach such a wide audience without all of you.

Friends and fellow authors—too many to name, but you know who you are—who lovingly support me with prayer and encouragement.

Andrea Mullins, publisher at New Hope Publishers. You've embraced my vision for books and Bible studies since the first day we met at AWSA and ICRS. Truly a God-ordained encounter.

Esteemed Endorsers—Drs. Les and Leslie Parrott; Janet Congo; Carole Lewis; Penny Monetti; Saundra Dalton-Smith, MD; Pam Farrel; Cindi McMenamin; Laura Petherbridge; Poppy Smith; Susan Titus Osborn; and Dawn Wilson.

My Lord and Savior, Jesus Christ, who continually keeps me *About His Work*!

PREFACE

THE WIFE OF A STAY-AT-HOME man is going to talk to God—a lot! Maybe she'll write a cathartic letter in her journal: *Dear God,* . . . Another wife might begin her pleading or thankful prayers with "Dear God, . . . " Still other wives in times of desperation or frustration cry out, "*Dear God, HE'S HOME!*"

Since my husband became a stay-at-home man, I regularly express each of those "Dear Gods," as do the wives submitting stories for this book. So don't feel guilty if you haven't always been joyous about this new closeness in your marriage relationship. And don't feel alone. When I sent out a request for stories of women with a husband home due to retirement, illness, disability, out of work, home office, the military . . . the stories flowed into my inbox and my ears.

Whenever I mention the title of this book, wives smirk with raised eyebrows and knowingly remark, "Boy, do I have a story for you!" "I need this book." "I know someone who could use this book." Or "I'm going to need this book soon, write fast!" I don't have to tell you the reasons for these responses because you've picked up this book or someone gave it to you.

Myriad emotions and reactions erupt from both spouses when an otherwise out-of-the-home-every-day husband is suddenly home all day—every day. Many wives have their own label for this occurrence. In *Honey, I'm Home for Good!*, Mary Ann Cook calls it spouse-in-the-house syndrome. Then there's retired-husband syndrome or military reintegration syndrome.

Every couple's response to their unique *syndrome* evolves from how they've dealt with previous transitions in their relationship. Couples who stumbled and fumbled without finding workable resolutions in the past, will probably stumble and fumble through this new situation too. However, couples who have successfully developed and implemented coping techniques may be better equipped to adjust to a full-time stay-at-home man. Even so, unexpected issues can blindside both spouses.

Life changes and progressions are part of God's plan—"There is a time for everything, and a season for every activity under the heavens"

(Ecclesiastes 3:1), even a time for a stay-at-home-man season. A spectrum of circumstances can initiate this change of season.

My husband and I are baby boomers in the transitional season of retirement. Boomers are a generation refusing to grow old. We throw away *AARP: The Magazine* and membership forms arriving in the mail and proudly announce, "Sixty is the new 40!" as if denial could alter the march of time.

Foresighted boomers prepared for their financial future—anticipating the glorious days of no alarm clocks and still being young enough to enjoy retirement. Still others didn't plan financially for retirement, or lost what they did have in the economic meltdown. Some had to take early retirement, or were part of a company downsizing or layoff, before they were ready.

Illness or injury isn't something anyone wants to consider or anticipate, at any age. Maybe couples took precautionary measures financially with insurance and savings, or not, but many expected the husband would be a strong, virile provider . . . as long as necessary. Then one day he's not working anymore, maybe for a short time, maybe forever. That's not right! The Bible says man should be toiling the fields and bringing home the bread (Genesis 3:17–19), which many interpret as, "until retirement." Disability or illness can also usher in a new season.

Or maybe one day your husband came home early from work holding a box with the contents of his desk and you knew without a word spoken that he would be out of work for a while. How do you comfort him through your own fear of wondering, *How will we survive financially and emotionally?*

Perhaps your husband's company wants him to work from home, or he's decided to take the plunge into self-employment and set up shop in the spare bedroom or garage. *Wasn't he supposed to go slay dragons during the day and return in the evening with provision?*

If your husband is in the military, or a job that regularly takes him away from home, you experience a revolving season of saying good-bye and then fitting him back into the home routine—*reintegration.*

My husband and I have been through each of these stay-at-home man scenarios—except for the military, but we have a married, career-military son, so we understand the life.

Whatever circumstances brought your husband home, most couples admit they didn't prepare for a time of being together 24/7! Regardless of the reason for this season, wives of stay-at-home men experience similar difficulties, hardships, and blessings. We're going to explore this kinship in a universal guide for living happily ever after with your stay-at-home man.

I'm certainly not an expert with all the answers, but together we can mentor and help each other. Through laughter and tears, frustrations and fears, we'll march arm-in-arm toward a common goal: keeping our marriages intact and our hearts right with God and our husbands, until we can say with thanksgiving and praise, "*Dear God, He's Home!*"

About His Work,

Janet

INTRODUCTION

My purpose in writing is simply this: that you who believe in God's Son will know beyond the shadow of a doubt that you have eternal life, the reality and not the illusion. — 1 JOHN 5:13 (*The Message*)

I HAVE A WINDOW INTO your life with a stay-at-home man. I want to walk beside you as only friends who have been in your shoes can. My desire is to mentor and encourage you from my experiences and to wrap you in God's goodness, peace, and love. While I may not know your name, I know your heart.

Dear God, He's Home! is a companion guide for wherever you are in your marriage or faith journey. I trust this book also will be an oasis of solace, comfort, and encouragement from God's Word as you seek and find God's purpose in the midst of your journey. For each of you, God's plan and purpose will be different and unique, but rest assured, He does have a plan. Nothing happens by accident in a believer's life. If we know God as our personal Savior, *"We know that God causes all things to work together for good to those who love God, to those who are called according to His purpose"* (Romans 8:28 NASB).

WHERE TO BEGIN?

This is your book to use in ways that serve you best. You might want to go through it on your own, with your husband, or with a group of other wives or couples with stay-at-home husbands using the study guide on page 188 and the "For Discussion" section at the end of each chapter.

Throughout the book, I recount my husband, Dave's, and my journey through "Dear God" journal entries, and other wives contribute their experiences on a particular topic in the "A Wife Shares" section. The format of the book is:

THE TOPIC TITLE — A QUOTE AND A SCRIPTURE.

JANET'S **JOURNAL** — My "Dear God."

A WIFE SHARES — Contributing wives with a stay-at-home man share their journey. Occasionally, a stay-at home man shares. All stories are true, but some names are fictitious.

MENTORING MOMENT — Lessons learned, helpful tips, encouragement.

GOD'S LOVE LETTER TO YOU — Personalized, paraphrased Scripture. Write your name in the blanks provided.

LET'S PRAY — Praying with me.

YOUR LETTER TO GOD — Encouraging prompts and a place to journal your story.

FOR **DISCUSSION** — Questions or topics to discuss with your spouse or small/support group.

JOURNALING

ONE OF MY VISIONS FOR *Dear God, He's Home!* is for it to be a safe place to document an epic time in your life. Whether you've journaled regularly for years or this is your first time, there's freedom and healing in expressing your thoughts and feelings in writing. At the end of each chapter, you can journal your own "Dear God." You may also want to write more in a separate journal.

Comfort often evolves from talking about what's bothering us — or writing about it. Think of journaling as writing a letter to God. Not everyone understands, but God always understands and He is eager to hear from you. Regardless of your faith or religious persuasion, you matter to God and He will fill the pages by nudging you toward helpful things to journal. Maybe you'll remember a good time to laugh about or contemplate a different perspective of a hurtful incident. Some days you'll write pages; other days you won't feel like writing more than a sentence.

Journaling is personal. Don't feel you have to share what you write with anyone, including your husband. However, like the women and men who share their stories in this book, God might provide opportunities for you to mentor others with the wisdom and encouragement you've learned along the journey.

The best part about journaling is that God is ready to receive your words with a faithful, listening ear. He can take it all: the good, the bad, and the ugly. He beckons, *"Come to me, all you who are weary and burdened, and I will give you rest. Take my yoke upon you and learn from me, for I am gentle and humble in heart, and you will find rest for your souls. For my yoke is easy and my burden is light"* (Matthew 11:28–30).

JOURNALING TIPS

- Pray before you start.
- Write your heart. Let your pen flow with thoughts and feelings.
- Don't worry about grammar, spelling, or sounding articulate or spiritual.
- Think of journaling as writing a letter to, or a written conversation with, God.
- Date your entries.
- Reflect on my "Dear God" journal entries or "A Wife Shares" or a "Mentoring Moment."
- "Your Letter to God" has thought-provoking questions to get you started, but don't feel confined to answering them. Write whatever you want.
- Develop abbreviations and symbols only you understand.
- When it hurts, talk about it. When you're mad, cry out—God can take it.
- Express the good and joyful times too.
- Don't worry if the pen seems too heavy—journaling shouldn't make you feel guilty. When the time is right, you'll get back to it again.
- Record your prayer requests and God's answers in "Prayer and Praise Journal," page 187.

PERSONALIZING AND PRAYING SCRIPTURE

You can read *Dear God, He's Home!* as a devotional or as a small/support group study of how God's Word, the Bible, applies to your life and marriage. The Bible provides the counsel, direction, peace, and answers you seek. It's "a manual for living, for learning what's right and just and fair; to teach the inexperienced the ropes and give our young people a grasp on reality. There's something here also for seasoned men and women, still a thing or two for the experienced to learn—Fresh wisdom to probe and penetrate, the rhymes and reasons of wise men and women. Start with GOD" (Proverbs 1:3–7 *The Message*).

The Bible is your personal guide for life. *Nothing else* can fill the deep need and hole in your heart except God and His Word. Often in the "God's Love Letter to You" or "Let's Pray" sections, we'll pray personalized, paraphrased Scriptures. Try praying the following personalized Scripture:

> *Lord, teach us your ways, O LORD, that we may live according to your truth! Grant us purity of heart, so that we may honor you. With all our heart, we will praise you, O Lord our God. We will give glory to your name forever. Amen.*
> (Psalm 86:11–12 NLT; paraphrased)

Writing this book for you helped me love and appreciate my stay-at-home man more than I ever imagined possible and I hope reading it will do the same for you with your stay-at-home man.

My prayer for you:

"May He give you the desires of your heart and make all your plans succeed" (Psalm 20:4).

Chapter 1:

HE'S HOME!

If your marriage is difficult, it doesn't mean your marriage is bad.
It just means you're married. — GARY THOMAS

I remember God — and shake my head.
I bow my head — then wring my hands.
I'm awake all night — not a wink of sleep;
I can't even say what's bothering me.
I go over the days one by one, I ponder the years gone by.

— PSALM 77:3–5 (*The Message*)

Our Story

Space and time have been our biggest issues. — NANCY

If only my words were written in a book —
better yet, chiseled in stone! — JOB 19:23–24 (*The Message*)

I'D BEEN WAITING TO MEET a godly man for a long time. I was
a single parent for 17 years and my only daughter, Kim, was getting
ready to leave for college so it seemed like the perfect time for God to
bring "Mr. Right" into my life. Then there he was — tall, dark, tanned,
and handsome! I had joined a small group Bible study comprised of
career men and women from my church. During introductions, Dave
said he was divorced with three kids and was a regional manager for a
semiconductor company.

Bingo! I thought I knew exactly why God had me join this group. This
man had definite potential. Eventually, he asked me out. Love blossomed.
Six months later, we became "Hubby" and "Wiffy" and started on the
journey of blending our two families. Life was good. We both had two

well-paying, challenging careers, a nice home, great kids, and I started attending seminary. Dual incomes afforded us the freedom to travel, remodel our home, and provide our kids with a comfortable lifestyle.

Three years after our wedding, the last child left home so we agreed I could resign from my career and go into full-time lay ministry, starting the Woman to Woman Mentoring Ministry at our church—Saddleback Church in Lake Forest, California. Dave's job would support us nicely and provide benefits. The mentoring ministry was growing and we were enjoying the luxuries of an empty nest . . . for all of three months. Then Dave was part of a corporate layoff five months after his 50th birthday.

"No problem," he said confidently. "I've never had trouble finding work. Recruiters are always contacting me with jobs from the best companies."

A "Job Placement Program" was part of his severance package, so for the next three months not much changed. Every morning he showered and shaved, dressed in his suit, starched shirt, tie, and dress shoes, grabbed his briefcase, and went to the "office" of the job placement company. I continued attending seminary and growing the Woman to Woman Mentoring Ministry.

Slightly daunted, but not discouraged when the three months ended with the job placement company and no jobs surfaced, Dave moved his recruiting efforts into one of the kids' vacated bedrooms, which we set up as his *temporary* office.

As the months dragged on, I could hear his frustrated, borderline-begging phone conversations. He was overqualified for any entrance opportunity and too old and high-paid for advanced positions. Discouragement turned into depression as my former corporate businessman in three-piece suits and shined designer shoes deteriorated into a couch potato in shorts, a tank top, and flip flops.

Watching him sink into a "midlife crisis," I convinced him to start working out at the local gym, where he actually found his next job after 18 months of unemployment. I did have to ask if it was a *job* or a *hobby* since it was working for a man with a small golf manufacturer's rep business who overheard Dave lamenting about his out-of-work dilemma while pumping iron at the gym. The "job" had no benefits and was commission only, but Dave loved being around golf courses for the next four years.

Just as he was starting to make a suitable living at this venture, his boss let him go, saying he couldn't afford to keep him on staff. This layoff coincided with my first breast cancer diagnosis. Again, Dave was back to recruiters, job fairs, scouring the newspaper . . . anything . . . nothing. Only this time, we couldn't afford for him to go into a depression or sit on the couch—Dave needed a job with benefits ASAP.

I was still working out of my home office leading the Woman to Woman Mentoring Ministry and had started About His Work Ministries—my writing and speaking ministry. Christian speakers and authors often receive the advice, "Never quit your day job." Too late—I *had* quit my day job. Now I had cancer and my husband was out of work, again.

Four months later, Dave came home from a job fair announcing he had an interview with a bug and termite exterminator company. I couldn't imagine Mr. Corporate America and golf rep Dave wearing a khaki green uniform, mask, hard hat, and work boots chasing bugs in attics, crawl spaces under houses, and around yards. But that's exactly what he did for the next seven years . . . until he couldn't walk anymore.

His right ankle began swelling, then he was limping, and finally the doctor said he eventually wouldn't be able to walk without having reconstructive foot surgery, which would require being off his feet at home for six-months to a year. His company gave him six months to return to work or lose his job.

A "six-month recovery" morphed into a year—unemployed again—but this time he was 64 and disabled. To Dave it was a no-brainer—retire. To me it was a brain-twister—retire? I fought it, denied it, tried to persuade him to find a desk job and work at least until he was 67 or 70 . . . but not retire. No, not stay home! How would we survive financially? What would he do with his time? How could I write with him around when I needed complete solitude?

In this book, I'll share with you how we worked through each of our "Dear God, He's Home!" seasons, as I let you peek into my heart and soul.

Your Story

"Hi, honey, I'm home! . . . And thanks to this baby [a fax machine], I'm home for good," he announced with a grin. "I'll be able to telecommute from home and avoid that awful freeway commute. I may even have time to do some consulting work on the side."

This surprise announcement of his intent to work from home caused me to drop the platter I was holding. As I stared at the broken chunks of china and mounds of ground beef splattered across the floor, I thought, *My life — like that platter — will never be the same again.*

And it hasn't. — MARY ANN COOK (*Honey, I'm Home for Good!*)

I will tell of the kindnesses of the LORD, the deeds for which he is to be praised, according to all the LORD has done for us—yes, the many good things he has done for the house of Israel, according to his compassion and many kindnesses. — ISAIAH 63:7

YOUR LETTER TO GOD

OK, it's your turn. What's your story? How do you happen to have a stay-at-home man? What are your concerns? Explain it all to God:

Dear God,   *Date:*

_____

_____

_____

_____

_____

_____

_____

_____

_____

_____

_____

_____

_____

FOR **DISCUSSION**

1. Describe your stay-at-home man scenario.

2. What emotions are you currently experiencing?

3. Why are you reading this book and how do you hope it will help your situation?

Chapter 2:

PARALYZING SHOCK

Most professionals wish to chart the course of their work life and subsequent retirement. Alan was no exception. Not yet ready to hang up his stethoscope, certainly not forced to do so, he worked half-days after recovering from bilateral pulmonary emboli and venous thrombosis, but he fizzled by noon. The anxiety over the fragility of life hit him hard. Funny how you never think it will be you, even when you see it on a daily basis. If his health had held out, we're both sure he'd still be working, even at 70. — NANCY

Stand in shock, heavens, at what you see! Throw up your hands in disbelief—this can't be! — JEREMIAH 2:12 (*The Message*)

You're What?

After raising eight children, I was looking forward to some empty-nester *me* time. When my husband announced he was taking an early retirement, I thought, *"Oh no! Now I have another one . . . "* — ANITA

It is a land as dark as midnight, a land of utter gloom where confusion reigns and the light is as dark as midnight. —JOB 10:22 (NLT)

JANET'S JOURNAL

Dear God,

After only 3 years of wedded bliss, we encountered our first stay-at-home saga. When Dave turned 50, he started worrying about his job being tenuous. I reassured him that he certainly didn't look 50, and how would they even know? He said, "Oh, they know, and I think we should prepare ourselves." I didn't take his advice. I resigned from my career to go into full-time lay ministry and reveled in having my husband supporting me after working 17 years as a single mom.

The "reveling" only lasted three months! One morning I got a surprise phone call from him asking for prayer. I thought he might be having second thoughts about our new couch arriving that day! He assured me he loved the couch but had received a fax announcing company layoffs, and his boss was coming to his office at 4:00 that afternoon, either to give him a bigger territory, or the boot.

Sure enough, at 5:00 he walked in the house carrying a box of his office possessions with the family picture from his desk peeking out the top—I couldn't believe it! They gave him 30 minutes to pack up his office, a three-month severance package, and a have-a-good life good-bye. Cold. Brutal.

Lord, how could this happen? Didn't you want me to go into ministry? Wasn't Dave supposed to support us while I served You? Will he get another job soon like he expects? How is this all going to turn out?

So many unanswered questions. Too late to take back the new couch . . .

In shock, Janet

A WIFE **SHARES**: *Char*

I'm living my perfect life, I thought as I sat at my computer. I'd just received a writing contract, which would enable me to continue working out of my home during our son John's sophomore year of high school. I hoped to replenish the family's savings account after helping fund a family reunion earlier that year.

I was grateful, knowing I couldn't do what I did without my husband, Richard's, support. His position as computer network manager had provided us with financial stability and health benefits while I worked as a freelance writer to supplement our income during our son's growing-up years. I was a very lucky woman.

My concentration was interrupted by John yelling, "Dad's home." It was only 3:00 P.M. Richard never came home at 3:00. He must be sick. I reached the front door just as he opened it. My heart leapt to my throat as I saw him enter the house holding his office plant and coffee mug. I didn't really need his explanation, "I've been laid off."

A STAY-AT-HOME MAN **SHARES**: *Joseph*

The phone call caught me off guard. It was shortly after 5:00 P.M. and I was beginning to slow down after a busy afternoon. When I recognized the voice, my pulse quickened. I knew the message couldn't be good. My caller, a Veterans Administration physician, calmly told me I had Agent Orange.

MENTORING MOMENT

Even though it's been 17 years since Dave's first layoff, I can still remember where we were when he told me he was worried about turning 50, and I can visualize myself vacuuming where the new couch was going to go when I got Dave's phone call. Laid off, downsized, fired, let go . . . whatever terminology, the result is the same—unemployment—scary and shocking for our husbands, our family, and us.

Maybe the shocking news that brought your husband home to stay was a medical diagnosis, an injury or accident, forced early retirement, your home turned into his office, or he's returning from deployment maybe with injuries or PTSD—whatever turned your world upside down, it calls for a response.

Webster's dictionary defines *shock*: "A sudden or violent disturbance of the mind, emotions, or sensibilities. Synonym 'startle' implies the sharp surprise of sudden fright." Our body reacts with dry mouth, racing heart, sinking stomach, sweaty palms, numbness, flushed face, maybe fainting or sickness—a terrible feeling. We can't live in a state of shock for long without our body completely shutting down. Mercifully, the shock phase passes and myriad reactions follow—denial, anger, depression, and eventually, acceptance.

GOD'S **LOVE LETTER** TO YOU

Dear _____,

I am holding you by your right hand—I, the Lord your God. And I say to you, "Do not be afraid. I am here to help you" (Isaiah 41:13 NLT; paraphrased).

Your Shock Absorber, God

LET'S **PRAY**

God, we're reeling from shock . . . numb. We need comfort and reassurance that somehow we'll make it through this. Help us process the news we've heard and accept the things we cannot change. We believe You are in this with us and You have a plan. Lord, let the love we have for our husbands draw us closer to them when they need us the most. Grow our love and don't allow anything to divide our marriages. We need You, Lord. We can't get through this without You. Amen.

This Can't be Happening to Us!

It's SCARY with a capital S C A R and Y!   — DEBORAH

If the Lord is with us, why has all this happened to us?
                                                    — JUDGES 6:13

JANET'S **JOURNAL**

Dear God,

Dave was so sure he'd quickly find another job. In the past, recruiters were always calling him, but it's been months and still no job. The rejection is taking a toll, and I can see depression consuming him. Sometimes he just sits on the couch . . . tousled hair, a week's growth on his face . . . staring into space . . . . What happened to the professional man I married?

The Woman to Woman Mentoring Ministry is soaring, and churches are calling to ask what we're doing. I can't go down this dark road of depression with him, so I've decided to write a resource to help churches start their own mentoring ministries. I know so little about computer graphics and design. Maybe engaging Dave in helping me with this project would give him purpose and he'd feel useful again. For now, we still have my insurance sales residuals and our savings. Something good has to come from this stressful time . . . I know it will!

Making the best of it, Janet

A WIFE **SHARES**: *Char*

With Richard's layoff, I knew I wouldn't be helping replenish the family's savings account. I'd be using the money for groceries and John's high school expenses. While I tried to be positive, other financial worries bubbled to the surface. Both Richard and I were driving vehicles with over 100,000 miles. Our plan was to get a car for John once he got his license, but that's out of the question now. The house needed several repairs, including a new air-conditioning unit. We'd have to come up with John's college tuition in a couple of years and there was the issue of saving for retirement.

I kept a text file of Isaiah 41:10 minimized on my computer screen. When anxiety crept up, I'd maximize the file and read the verse a few times. It was wonderfully reassuring.

A STAY-AT-HOME MAN **SHARES**: *Joseph*

As I hung up the phone, a flood of emotions overwhelmed me. *I had Agent Orange. Why now?* I had lived a life defying odds at every turn, often overcoming barriers of adversity. Now, the supreme test was at hand. I desperately needed the presence of God to calm my shattered nerves and brace me for the journey ahead. Yes, I needed a God who had sometimes seemed important, if inconvenient. He was a force to propel me through the upcoming darkness.

MENTORING MOMENT

Something good did come out of Dave being home. With both of us unemployed, people asked when I was going back to work and Dave would reply, "Janet's about the Lord's work." About His Work Ministries became the name of my writing and speaking ministry, which Dave helped launch while teaching me how to compose and format on the computer—something I never thought possible. God used this time of secular unemployment to keep Dave God-employed with me.

Whatever brought your husband home didn't catch God off guard. When your husband is feeling weak, he needs you to remain strong—that kind of strength only comes from God and reading His Word. Spend extra time with God and maintain your "normal" schedule. God will find a way where there seems to be no way—as long as you trust and obey and look for Him at work in the midst of your circumstances.

GOD'S **LOVE LETTER** TO YOU

*Dear*_____,

I'm telling you, "You're my servant, serving on my side. I've picked you. I haven't dropped you." Don't panic. I'm with you. There's no need to fear, for I'm your God. I'll give you strength. I'll help you. I'll hold you steady, keep a firm grip on you (Isaiah 41:9–10 *The Message*; paraphrased).

> *Never Leaving or Forsaking You,*
> *God*

LET'S **PRAY**

Oh Lord, having a husband home is something we thought only happened to other women! Not only is it a hardship, we fear it's going to put a real strain on our marriages. Help us stay calm and not panic. Give us supportive, encouraging, and understanding hearts. We need to be strong now for our husbands and the family, but we feel so weak. Please provide us with supernatural strength that others will know can only come from You. May You get all the glory. Amen.

We'll Be Fine

Our biggest challenge is reintegration after deployment, but we made a commitment when we became engaged that divorce would never be an option. — SHERRY

Don't waver in resolve. Don't fear. Don't hesitate. Don't panic. God, your God, is right there with you, fighting with you against your enemies, fighting to win. — DEUTERONOMY 20:1 (*The Message*)

JANET'S **JOURNAL**

Dear God,

I always believed You would see us through unemployment trials, so I focused on all the wonderful things happening in the mentoring ministry—lives changing for the better. I knew our lives would get better too, I just couldn't see how or when.

After 18 long, painful months, Dave finally found a job as a manufacture's rep for golf clothes and accessories—minimal pay, no benefits, long hours, and we had to invest in a van! But Dave looked so happy every morning dressed in his name-brand golf clothes—one "benny" of the job—on his way to one of his favorite places—golf courses. It was hard not to be happy for him. Although, I often lamented whether this was a job or a hobby—whatever. It got him out of the house, and we'd keep making do until he started making money.

Then just when this "job" finally started to pay off after four years, Dave's boss let him go while I was in the midst of breast cancer treatment. Could it get any worse?

Lord, You are so good, You never let us down. This time, unemployment only lasted four months and Dave was back to work as a termite inspector, trading in his golf clothes for a company-issued uniform, hard hat, and pickup. Thank You, Lord, for a husband willing to do whatever it takes to support us.

Depending on You, Janet

A WIFE SHARES: *Char*

"Oh, we'll be OK," was all I could think to say. I said it more to reassure our son John than myself, but it wasn't long before panic set in.

Richard began enumerating our options as we sat at the kitchen table with a pile of paperwork, a calculator, and two cups of green tea. "A severance package will take us through the end of the year. Then, I'll get unemployment and we qualify for COBRA." We'd be all right for a little while—long enough for Richard to find full-time work.

Or so we thought.

Richard began an intense search for another professional position in network management while I continued with my contract job. I was happy for the work as a distraction from worry.

A STAY-AT-HOME MAN SHARES: *Joseph*

I'm a fighter; I'll never give up until the last breath. A lesson I hope my three young children can take from me, especially if I meet an early death from Agent Orange side effects. Can I forgive their mother, who abandoned us for medical school and a man young enough to be my son? Where was the "in sickness and health" promise we made at our wedding? It really doesn't matter, because I have to manage the hand I'm dealt—a sick, at-home, single parent.

MENTORING MOMENT

When our husbands are in a precarious position, out of work—temporary or permanent—ill, disabled, changing job surroundings, home from a difficult deployment, or anything that sets his and our world on end, we wives have a choice. Will we be an enabler, encourager, endorser, edifier—or a deserter? Sadly, some women run at the first indication of happily ever after turning into imperfect and real.

I'm not proud of some of my reactions at various times in Dave's stay-at-home seasons, and other times I amazed myself at how calm and optimistic I could remain in the midst of our crises. During discouraging "Eeyore" moments, I reminded myself that God knew what was happening and maybe He was working on something in my husband's or my life. If I tried to be a "fixer" or take matters into my own hands, we might have to experience this all over again.

I had to learn to let go of my concerns and sincerely believe everything would be fine if we turned it *all* over to God. Little did I know that surrender would eventually result in, "Yeah, I'm home forever!" sooner than I expected.

GOD'S LOVE LETTER TO YOU

*Dear*_____,

"So this is what the Sovereign Lord says: 'See, I lay a stone in Zion, a tested stone, a precious cornerstone for a sure foundation; the one who relies on it will never be stricken with panic'" (Isaiah 28:16).

Watching Over You, God

LET'S PRAY

Abba Father, we want to believe everything is going to be OK, but we still can't dispel chilling doubts. We push our husbands to change the situation when we know we should be talking more with You and relying on You to work out Your good and perfect will. Help us stay focused on Your promises and not our circumstances. Enable us to be a helpmate to our husbands and not a hindrance. We need You, Lord. Please stay close by our sides. Amen.

YOUR LETTER TO GOD

This might have been a difficult chapter as you relived past pains or current issues. Healing and comfort come when you put your feelings into words and pour them out on paper. Tell everything to God here:

Dear God,   *Date:*

_____

_____

_____

_____

_____

_____

_____

_____

FOR DISCUSSION

1. Describe your reactions to learning your husband would be home full-time.

2. What were your worst fears?

3. How do you feel now about your husband being home?

Chapter 3:
ADJUSTING PLANS

Adjustments, transitions, more time to spend together again—to make it work—pray individually and together. Ask the Lord for joy. Spend time in God's Word and make sure there's nothing in your life hindering this stage from being the kind of life we dream about.

— ELIZABETH

I have heard all about you, Lord,
    in addition, I am filled with awe by the amazing things you
    have done.
In this time of our deep need, begin again to help us,
    as you did in years gone by.
Show us your power to save us.   — HABAKKUK 3:2 (NLT)

Game Changer

Dealing with unemployment hadn't been part of our plan. Every penny of expected income was earmarked for family needs.   — CHAR

We humans keep brainstorming options and plans, but GOD's purpose prevails.   —PROVERBS 19:21 (*The Message*)

JANET'S JOURNAL

Dear God,

A feeling of impending dread and anxiety eclipsed me as we sat in the doctor's office discussing Dave's impending reconstructive right foot surgery. Dave wouldn't be weight bearing for a minimum of six months postsurgery and *might* be able to return to work then. He had switched jobs from termite inspector to pest control technician, which required walking, standing, and climbing up and down hills. The doctor was encouraging him to look for different work. I could sense Dave's thoughts: *Who's going to hire a 64-year-old man who can't walk?*

I gave him the look: *Push those thoughts out of your mind.* "Our plan" was for Dave to work until at least 67 to qualify for full Social Security, and I'd be eligible for Medicare. With my breast cancer history, we need health insurance benefits. He *has* to go back to work in six months, the time his company allows for medical disability. One day more would be termination—definitely not in the plan!

As Dave and the doctor continued talking, I scanned my calendar trying to determine when we could squeeze in surgery between my four book deadlines due in the next 10 months and several out-of-town speaking engagements. Then I heard Dave tell the doctor he wanted surgery *next* month! What?

The doctor continued: After surgery Dave would be in bed for at *least* a month, then using a knee scooter, wheelchair, and crutches. I visualized me doing *all* the driving, cooking, shopping, errands, cleaning, household chores—things I had difficulty managing with one book deadline, not to mention four—oh yes, and caring for a housebound, bedbound husband!

Lord, can I do this? Is it even possible?

The room went silent as the doctor and Dave looked over at me, probably wondering why I was pale, dazed, and asking for a glass of water. We needed a new plan and we needed one fast.

Feeling overwhelmed, Janet

A WIFE **SHARES:** *Trudy*

My husband drove a bulldozer for 30 years. When the economy worsened, there was no work, so he had to "retire." We were shell-shocked; it was a real game changer! Then it became this amazing blessing. He actually couldn't, and shouldn't, have been working as hard as he was anyway. So I went to work and he took over the household duties, along with taking care of the dogs and yard. He loves it.

Now he is so appreciative of all I did for him. When he used to take a bath after work—he loves his baths—he left a three-inch dirt ring around the tub, which he never noticed I had to clean. Now that he's the "housecleaner" he says, "I can't believe you did this all those years without complaining, without pay."

I used to lie in bed at night wondering how I would pay the bills if he couldn't work, but now *I'm* paying the bills. Fifty-eight wasn't too old to learn a new trade, which I love — teaching quilting.

MENTORING MOMENT

If a husband coming home to stay isn't in the plan, or even if it is, the focus is usually on the logistical and financial implications, not the emotional ramifications. Many of us didn't consider or anticipate the relational impact of this "game changer" until *after* it rocked our world.

I wish Dave and I had taken the time to sit down and discuss possible outcomes of our game changers, or had a tool to help anticipate the repercussions. I developed such a tool for you based on what would have helped us and I hope helps you. In "Sanity Tools" on page 179–180, you'll find guidelines for making decisions and developing a plan, along with a peacekeeping work sheet and a place to develop your plan. Your "new plan" just might turn out to be a blessing in disguise, as Trudy and her husband discovered.

GOD'S LOVE LETTER TO YOU

Dear _____,

"I know what I'm doing. I have it all planned out — plans to take care of you, not abandon you, plans to give you the future you hope for" (Jeremiah 29:11 *The Message*).

Your Life-Planner, God

LET'S PRAY

Lord, a change in plans is difficult when there are so many unknowns. We don't know what the future holds, be we do know Who holds our future. Guide us as we prepare to go down this new road in uncharted territory. Help us stay in one accord with our husbands and with You. Amen.

Switching Roles

I'm sure many women find it challenging — and yet, rewarding — to have their husbands retire while they're still working. It's discouraging when I'm working long hours to meet a deadline and he's sitting at his computer playing games or watching his favorite sports. Before I have a meltdown, he thoughtfully offers to run to the store and cook dinner or make reservations at our favorite restaurant. —SUSAN

Too much change, too fast, and they were scared.

—LUKE 8:37 (*The Message*)

JANET'S JOURNAL

Dear God,

I sense our lives are in for a BIG change in *every* area. We started our marriage with both of us as "bread winners." Then we agreed I would quit and go into full-time ministry and Dave would support us—which had several setbacks—but he always found something to bring in "the bread," while I continued in ministry.

Now with his upcoming foot surgery, what will happen if he can't work . . . ever again? For the immediate future, I'll be doing *everything*. How long will this last? If I have to take on more speaking engagements and write more books to keep us afloat, how will I do everything else too?

Times, they are a-changin'—we're not only reversing roles, I'm taking on *all* the roles! I hope I'm ready.

Resisting change, Janet

A WIFE SHARES: *Deola*

My husband was a police officer, and I was a stay-at-home, homeschooling mom for 17 years. My husband suffered a torn rotator cuff during a tactical training exercise and didn't regain full mobility of his shoulder to perform all his duties.

A desk job wasn't an option, so we had no choice—my husband retired at age 41. I had a dormant PhD in psychology, so he asked me to return to work. I found a job teaching at a local university, the children went back to school, and he became the stay-at-home husband.

We started talking about how our roles would change a month or two before I started working again. *Every* household duty needed adjustment. Would I continue paying the bills or would he? Who would make dinner? How would the house get clean?

31

He volunteered first to do the cooking, but didn't want to take it on until he *absolutely* had to. But once he got his hands on an oven mitt and a spatula, he was unstoppable. He loves cooking and is even considering cooking school.

Handling the finances became an immediate issue. I had always paid the bills and managed our money. I attempted to show him my routine: bank passwords, bill due dates, amounts owed, etc. That task fell back into my lap right away.

So we've had to adjust. New issues come up all the time. Right now, it's completing the taxes. That's my job. My husband continues with the jobs he's always had like toy fixer, wrestler, and popcorn maker, along with new duties—errand runner, grocery shopper, dentist and doctor appointment maker, and taxi driver—my old jobs. Now, I'm the "breadwinner," the one who misses sports games and sometimes isn't home for dinner.

It's hard changing roles. Many, I'd love to have the chance to do again. I'm fortunate, though, because I'm a teacher. When summer comes, I'll take over many of those jobs again—at least for a short time.

MENTORING MOMENT

The one thing we can expect in this world is change. The weather changes, a phone call can change everything, people change, kids grow up and change, seasons change . . . life evolves. Yet many of us cling to the known, fatally resisting change.

Role reversals are a *huge* change, and one we're often ill equipped to accept. When a husband comes home full-time, the wife may become the sole provider—hopefully the husband can, and will, fill the void at home.

When a husband becomes ill or disabled, the wife catapults into taking on many, or all, of his home responsibilities—ready or not.

Military wives experience switching roles every time husbands leave and return. In *Called to Serve*, Lt. Col. Tony Monetti and Penny Monetti describe what many families experience when the husband comes home:

> The second wave of transition gushes in like an unexpected tsunami . . . a role reversal suddenly occurs. Returning soldiers long to reclaim the captain's seat while wingmen [wives] are used to piloting the family jet solo.

Veola, in the above "A Wife Shares," and her husband anticipated and discussed the repercussions of their role switching. You'll read later that even with this groundwork, they still had issues—it's an ongoing process settling into roles different than you've experienced most of your married life.

Like all the adjustments encircling husbands becoming a stay-at-home man, our attitude determines how smoothly a role change occurs. See if you can pick up some tips from how Susan (from the opening quote) and her retired husband make the role reversal work for them:

- My husband is a tremendous help keeping the records for my business (a task I detest), editing my writing, and running errands.
- I speak at conferences, and he goes with me and runs my book table or helps with the event.
- He installed a generator in our fifth-wheel trailer, so even when nestled in the woods or sitting by the ocean at a state park, I can still work—no interruptions or household duties calling. Even though we're sharing a tight space, the beauty of nature and no TV keep my husband quiet. He works on his crossword puzzles while I type away. It makes for a great arrangement.

GOD'S **LOVE LETTER** TO YOU

Dear _____,

Then I the LORD *God said, "It is not good for the man to be alone. I will make a helper who is just right for him"* (Genesis 2:18 NLT; paraphrased).
Your Helper, God

LET'S **PRAY**

Oh Lord, we liked the way things were and we liked our roles before our husbands came home. We're trying to be flexible and flow with the changes, but it's going to require a sacrifice and change of attitude on our part. Give us bendable, humble hearts and show us how to make life better for our husbands, who are making a big change too. Amen.

Working as a Team

"Being on the same team" reminds me that God has joined us together in marriage to work together serving God for a common purpose.

— PENNY MONETTI, *Called to Serve*

Submit to one another out of reverence for Christ.

—EPHESIANS 5:21

JANET'S JOURNAL

Dear God,

Dave and I prayed to You for strength and direction and decided I would go to our mountain cabin in Idyllwild and write for the month before his scheduled surgery. Write I did and completed one book.

Dave's surgery went well, and after a night in the hospital, he came home with an ice pack machine that needed filling and emptying several times a day, a regime of pills, follow-up doctor appointments, and *complete* immobility. The first few weeks he slept a lot, so in between meeting his needs, I wrote.

As he began feeling better and could sit up in bed, I brought him a lap table (which I bought in anticipation of this day), a laptop computer, and a red pen and set him to work editing my manuscripts and working through the Bible studies I was writing. I put lunch in a cooler by his bed, filled up his water jug and ice machine, and told him to call me on his cell phone if he needed anything *really* important between trips downstairs from my office to check on him.

Working it out, Janet

A WIFE SHARES: Kathy

With us both working together at home, we're still working out the best routine for the household chores. We do laundry and housecleaning together; I do most of the grocery shopping, meal planning, and cooking. Russ loads the dishwasher, and I wash the pans. Russ runs most of the errands like banking, paying bills, and going to the post office. He also takes care of lawn care and the cars. I'm working more office hours than him, so he's willing to take up the slack on some of the household tasks.

MENTORING MOMENT

One morning while marinating lamb chops I had defrosted for dinner, Dave was sitting in his recliner reading the newspaper, still in his PJs at 10:00 A.M. I was hurrying to get back to work on a book deadline, when it hit me: few men wake up in the morning wondering, *What should we have for dinner?*

When hubby is working all day, it seems a fair division of efforts — you plan and make dinner, he goes to work to pay for it. Now that he's home, it's time to discuss a redistribution of household tasks *before* you become resentful. Otherwise, when he asks how your day is going, or what's for dinner, he won't understand why you give him the cold shoulder. Believe me when I say, husbands are clueless. You need to open the discussion on teamwork.

As I marinated those lamb chops, I thought, *I'll have him barbeque them and put some veggies and bread on the grill. I won't have to cook and have the mess to clean up. That's teamwork.* I love Anita's advice to her daughters: "Never figure out how to use the barbecue. That's the only freedom you'll ever have from cooking." I've taken that advice myself, especially at Thanksgiving when we barbecue the turkey — what a blessing!

Whether or not you planned for having a stay-at-home husband, it's imperative to now pool efforts and work together as the team you became on your wedding day. Help your husband become part of the solution instead of looking at him as the problem. If he isn't physically able to pitch in and help with meals, order in, do take out, or go out when you feel you need a break from preparing meals. Find ways for him to help within his areas of expertise and capabilities.

Few husbands come up with ideas on their own, so be creative and courteous with your suggestions. Dave doesn't cook, but he now sets the table, empties the dishwasher, does the dishes, takes out the trash, occasionally stirs a pot on the stove, and is great at barbequing.

His real forte is helping me in the ministry with his computer and technical skills — something he's good at and enjoys. So I'll make the dinners if he'll publish the newsletter, update the Web site, create power points, make business cards, edit my books . . . .

Submit every day to the Lord. Pray about your schedule and your plans and embrace each day as an opportunity to try something new and hold up your end of the team. Priscilla said that, with money tighter when her husband retired, she went to the library instead of buying a book.

If you're a military wife with a husband returning from deployment, you're other half is returning to complete you and he understands teamwork—it means survival. He has trained in how to go into new situations with his team and accomplish a goal under harrowing circumstances. Ask him to teach you some of those teambuilding skills and talk together about how to apply them to your marriage.

GOD'S **LOVE LETTER** TO YOU

*Dear*_____,

"The one who plants and the one who waters work together with the same purpose. And both will be rewarded for their own hard work" (1 Corinthians 3:8 NLT).

On Your Team, God

LET'S **PRAY**

Lord, we want to make this work. Keep us humble and willing to compromise. Remove from our minds any "poor me" or martyr attitudes. Help us develop teamwork skills and focus on what's best for *both* of us, not just ourselves. Thank You, Father. Amen.

Our Plan Isn't Working!

With my husband retired, it's definitely twice the husband and half the money.

— PRISCILLA

Job answered God: "I'm convinced: You can do anything and everything. Nothing and no one can upset your plans."

—JOB 42:1–2 (*The Message*)

JANET'S JOURNAL

Dear God,

I actually made progress in my writing while Dave was bedridden, but when he became semimobile, the peace and quiet vanished. Enjoying the new freedom, he started tearing—well it sounded like that anyway—through the house on his knee scooter and crutches or sat at his desk with his leg propped up on the shredding machine, assailing me with questions—"When's dinner?" or "Whatcha doin'?"—whenever I came downstairs to use the bathroom. Lord, why didn't we put a bathroom in my office loft?

I almost had accidents waiting till the last minute to run downstairs because I didn't want my train of thought interrupted—remember I'm the kind of writer who "needs to be alone, darling."

Wife interrupted, Janet

A WIFE SHARES: *Shirley*

It had been our desire for such a long time to retire early and just be with each other! Well, God had a different plan for us and called me into a ministry position requiring travel and a home office. I really needed a quiet environment to do ministry work.

Always supportive of my ministry, my retired husband tried to be helpful and take care of many little details for me. But we needed to set some *space* rules, or I would never get any work done.

We came up with our plan: a closed office door meant I was working, so don't bother me. Picture this . . . my husband cracks the door open and looks in with one eye if he wants to talk to me. I can feel it when someone is watching me, so there goes my concentration and our plan.

MENTORING MOMENT

If you pray for God to direct your life, an interruption in your plans may be a "God intervention." God looks at the global picture, and *our* plans aren't always *His* plans. Adjusting to His plan usually requires creativity and flexibility.

Virelle said when her husband retired, the downsized four-room condo they moved to was their favorite home ever. However, she added, "I lost my office and have written two books sitting on the couch—bad for my back. My husband, who's normally quiet, talks all the time when I'm home. I love him dearly, but need quiet to write. My only solution is to take my computer to the library and use a private study room." Great idea!

Shirley, in the above "Wife Shares," worked through her "space" issues by arriving at healthy guidelines for all of us to consider:

I have to confess that in the past, my husband opening the door and peeking in while I was working would upset me. God has been teaching me ways to help with our "space rules":

- To accomplish true success, I must remember kindness rules. It's easy to show everyone else kindness and overlook the home front.
- I need realistic expectations. It takes patience and time to work out "*space* rules."
- If I'm having a self-centered moment, I stop and think about the value of our relationship.
- Peaceful living requires humility. I'm not the only one who has worth in my home.
- I know the *space* issue will always be around, but we've agreed not to allow anything to come between us for the sake of our relationship. That's what love does.

GOD'S **LOVE LETTER** TO YOU

*Dear*_____,

"*Jesus was blunt: 'No chance at all if you think you can pull it off by yourself. Every chance in the world if you let God do it'*" (Mark 10:27 *The Message*).

Your Helper, God

LET'S **PRAY**

Lord, this is harder than we thought. We made a plan with our husbands and we're trying to stick to it, but circumstances keep changing or things happen we didn't expect or plan. Some days it seems like this isn't going to work, but then You step in after we've prayed and turned it over to You, and somehow, everything works out for the best. Thank You! Amen.

Keeping the Peace

We settled into a routine—some of it's even positive! — NANCY

I've just made my peace offerings and fulfilled my vows.
— PROVERBS 7:14 (NLT)

JANET'S JOURNAL

Dear God,

I was desperate. We had to have a new plan. The book deadlines were closing in, and I was on the verge of "losing it." So after dinner one night, I asked Dave if we could discuss some "house rules" for when I was writing. I reminded him of my need for solitude when I write—which was also my "work." I explained that the looming deadlines, combined with the extra responsibility since his foot surgery and now driving him to physical therapy, were stirring up a perfect storm for a meltdown.

I had him laughing about almost having accidents from waiting so long to run downstairs to the bathroom, afraid he would want to chat or ask me questions. He said he understood and would close his "office" door and put a sticky note on it if he needed to talk with me about something important.

We also agreed that unless it was an emergency, he would save all his questions to discuss with me at dinner. I didn't know we were setting the groundwork for a permanent transition. For now, I just needed to meet my deadlines and keep the peace at home.

Peacefully, Janet

A WIFE SHARES: *Deborah*

The first few months after Ken's layoff, I was *anything* but poised and graceful or gracious. I was so terrified of what we might lose and at odds with Ken about what he felt God was calling him to do (starting his own business), that I'm afraid I was a terrible example of how to respond. When my husband needed my support and encouragement most, I failed him.

When he did finally start his own business out of the basement in our home, I struggled with him being home full-time when I already worked from home. Randomly during *my* workday, he would pop upstairs for a chat, to see what was for lunch or dinner, or just to ask how my day was going. My job requires deep concentration. This drove me a little crazy—OK, a lot crazy.

We've since been able to negotiate amicable terms. A key element of our now happy co-worker status is so simple it's almost comical. When I'm working and need silence and no interruptions, I hang a lantern at the top of the stairway. When my husband sees that lantern, he knows he's in a "no-fly" zone and his "water cooler" time will have to wait. I try very hard not to put the lantern up unless I really need uninterrupted work time. It keeps the peace.

MENTORING MOMENT

I hope you've started working on the peacekeeping work sheet in "Sanity Tools" on page 180 and are developing a plan together. You're not writing this plan in stone—it'll need revisiting as life happens—but it's a starting place. Keep your sense of humor and work on mutually agreeable solutions. Don't make this all about you. Ask where your husband needs you to accommodate his needs. Remember his life has just gone through a major change too and he's establishing a new life schedule for himself.

Military wife Diana concurs: "Something I think our soldiers struggle with when they get home is the fine line between being overwhelmed with the needs of the family and not feeling needed. Let your soldier know you need him in a loving, patient manner. Communicate . . . ask . . . don't assume anything."

If your marriage "worked" because your husband wasn't home full-time and you were busy raising the kids, it's time to work on your marriage, and that may be why God has given you this uninterrupted time together—don't waste it and don't regret it. Do embrace the opportunity and each other.

GOD'S LOVE LETTER TO YOU

Dear _____,

"Peace I leave with you; my peace I give you. I do not give to you as the world gives. Do not let your hearts be troubled and do not be afraid" (John 14:27).

Your Peacekeeper, God

LET'S **PRAY**

Abba Father, so many things have happened in our lives to upset the peace. Help us maintain a gentle and quiet spirit when we're talking to our husbands and give us patience when we disagree or don't see eye-to-eye. Remind us that our responses and the way we handle this situation are a witness—either good or bad—to those watching us, especially our family. Give us tools to live in peace with You and each other. Amen.

YOUR LETTER TO GOD

It's not easy grappling with a future different from your plans and dreams. Do you feel any clarity or are you still in a state of confusion? Let God give you a vision and a hope for your future.

Dear God,   *Date:*

_____

_____

_____

_____

_____

_____

_____

_____

_____

_____

_____

_____

_____

_____

_____

_____

_____

_____

_____

_____

_____

FOR **DISCUSSION**

1. What creative tips or ideas do you have for surviving life's "game changers"?

2. How is your marriage coping, and what have you learned so far that you could apply?

3. What changes are you willing to make to keep the peace?

Chapter 4:
ESTABLISHING A NEW NORMAL

In talking to many military wives, one of the biggest challenges of a loved one returning home is meeting him right where he's at and adjusting to the "new normal."   — KATHRYN

On that day the sources of light will no longer shine, yet there will be continuous day! Only the Lord knows how this could happen. There will be no normal day and night, for at evening time it will still be light.   —ZECHARIAH 14:6–7(NLT)

Help! Our Diversity is Showing

You're not going to tone down my Type-A, medically retired, physician husband. He doesn't understand why I don't have the passion for the same things he does. He's trying to get the eschatology of Revelation straight; I figure it's not something we'll ever really know in this life.

— NANCY

My husband doesn't realize we're different personalities. I enjoy working because I see results. He's primarily phlegmatic. I'm melancholy. Phlegmatics like to sit back and observe . . . they'd rather watch something than actually participate.   — PRISCILLA

A body isn't just a single part blown up into something huge. It's all the different-but-similar parts arranged and functioning together.   — 1 CORINTHIANS 12:14 (*The Message*)

JANET'S JOURNAL

Dear God,

You made Dave and me with opposite personalities, which often result in contrasting or opposing reactions to circumstances. Dave's a processor; I'm a producer. He's rational; I'm emotional. He's an introvert; I'm the extrovert. He moves slowly; I'm fast-paced. He's content to sleep in late; I feel that's a terrible waste. He unpacks his suitcase; I live out of my suitcase. And on and on it goes. . . . Often we balance out each other, but other times we bring out the worst in each other. It makes for exciting and explosive 24/7 life together.

Emotionally, Janet

A WIFE SHARES: *Kathy*

Russ left full-time church ministry and joined my company headquartered in our home. We've dealt with lots of dilemmas of both working out of the home. He's up early and works until mid-afternoon, then he's ready for a change of pace. I tuck in Russ at his bedtime (we have a nice goodnight ritual), and I stay up working another two-three hours so I sleep in a couple of hours later than Russ.

Our work routines differ. I like working from my laptop in my recliner with the TV on. Russ works from his desk in another room with an office set-up and music playing to block out my TV noise. Our struggle:

- Different work hours and work styles can be distracting during prime working time.
- Each thinks we work harder than the other does.
- No private *alone* time. Sometimes, I want to have a phone conversation with a girlfriend without him listening. We all need our own space occasionally. I'm sure he feels the same way.
- I sing, and it's awkward finding time to rehearse in private.

MENTORING MOMENT

While packing for a trip Dave asked me, "How many days are you packing for?" I looked at him quizzically and was speechless because I pack for the trip events—shoes, under garments, jewelry to go with an "outfit" for each occasion. Observing my blank expression, he further explained he was asking because he wanted to know how many pairs of socks and underwear to pack.

I burst out laughing. This was such a foreign concept to me. I load clothes into my suitcase until the lid won't close or I reach 50 pounds—the maximum for air travel—whichever comes first. His suitcase had neat, even rows of t-shirts, underwear, shirts, and socks for each day, to which he adds a couple pairs of jeans and a jacket; mine had clothes overflowing out the top with the lid only half closed. A revealing visual of our stark differences.

Even if you have similar personalities, God created men and women to be completely different creatures in communication styles and thought processes—and get this, wives, neither one is right or wrong. You don't really want your husband to be exactly like you, do you? That would be terribly boring!

God wired us differently on purpose—not to frustrate us, but to help us complete each other. I love this quote from Nancy Cobb and Connie Grigsby in their book *How to Get Your Husband to Listen to You*: "Being wired differently from you doesn't make your husband weird. It's what makes him a *man*."

Deb tells how their differences became cohesive and not divisive when her husband retired. Instead of complaining about the other one's habits, they make it work for them:

> We've learned to enjoy our differences. I'm a night owl—I like to stay up late and sleep late. He's an early bird—he loves to get up early. We enjoy the hours in between together, but each has our privacy when the other is asleep.

Dave and I committed to putting Jesus Christ at the center of our marriage. When our differences are showing and we find ourselves at opposite poles on a topic, the only way we reach an agreement is to stop, pray, and ask Jesus to show us His way.

GOD'S **LOVE LETTER** TO YOU

Dear _____,

Remember the fruit the Holy Spirit produces love, joy and peace. It is being patient, kind, and good. It is being faithful and gentle and having control of oneself (Galatians 5:22 NIrV; paraphrased).

Creator of Diversity, God

LET'S **PRAY**

Holy Spirit, help us be more like You . . . patient, kind, understanding, gentle . . . We want to celebrate and not exacerbate differences with our husbands. Teach us to appreciate the unique way You made each one of us. Restore harmony in our marriages. Amen.

This Is My Home

When my CEO husband retired, he started rearranging *my* kitchen!

— SANDY

She watches over the affairs of her household.

— PROVERBS 31:27 (TNIV)

JANET'S **JOURNAL**

Dear God,

When I quit my career in insurance and set up my ministry office in our home, the house became *my* space. If Dave decided to come home for lunch without telling me or stopped by to pick up something, I felt he should call before dropping by *my* workplace, as I would do before going to *his* office.

The times he was home with temporary unemployment or illness, I struggled with him invading *my* space. I need complete peace, quiet, and no distractions when I write and work. I also need *my* space to be neat and clean so I can move around freely without stumbling over misplaced items like shoes, briefcases, books, an open drawer or cupboard door. Dave is a self-described low-key "creature of comfort" — distractions or things out of place don't bother him.

It's now been six months since Dave's foot surgery and he's nowhere near ready to return to work. The severance papers are in the mail . . . he's out of work again . . . and this time I think he's home for good! I've lost my sanctuary. My home is not *my* space anymore. Oh yes, I hear You . . . this is Dave's home too . . . even during the day.

Not home alone, Janet

A WIFE **SHARES:** *Michelle*

I retired first and we moved into our mountain "retirement home." I loved being by myself during the day, fixing up the house and enjoying "my space." Two years later, my husband, Bob's, older brother had a bad fall and incurred injuries prohibiting him from ever fulfilling his retirement dreams. The accident was on a Friday and my Bob gave his resignation notice the following Monday! He realized he wasn't in charge of everything in his life and he wasn't going to let what happened to his brother happen to him.

This abrupt plunge into retirement left Bob not knowing what to do when a weekend was over and he didn't go to work. I had always looked at the house as *my* home, and then suddenly Bob was there *all* the time taking up *my* space, hovering over me and expecting me to entertain him.

He would sit on the edge of the bathtub while I was getting ready: I resorted to locking the bathroom door. I felt smothered and wanted to say, "Leave me alone!" One day I turned around at the kitchen sink and ran right into him. I said, "I love you dearly, but you *have* to find something to do with yourself!"

MENTORING MOMENT

Even if you planned your husband's homecoming for years or had advance warning, you can't anticipate the repercussions until you live through the experience. Many wives with a stay-at-home man recount the loss of *my* home, *my* space, *my* privacy, *my* domain, *my* downtime, a place to call *my* own. As if that weren't enough, looking for something to do with all his newfound free time, the husband may decide to rearrange *your* routine, *your* kitchen — *your* life!

He's trying to find *his* space in what used to be *your* space and that can lead to crowded space. Military families call this the "reentry phase" or reintegration — fitting back into "normal" home life and society. In *Called to Serve*, Lt. Col. Tony and Penny Monetti quote one returning solider who said he felt like "a background wall in his own home." An apt word picture for any stay-at-home man.

The home balance of authority feels off kilter when a husband is home. The Monettis give great advice that applies to all couples regardless of the homecoming circumstances: "This transitional period is short-lived if couples learn to communicate their feelings early on. One wife advises wingmen [wives] to seek their spouses' advice on small matters, as well as the crucial ones, to help returning spouses feel needed."

Try suggesting things for your husband to do that don't involve rearranging "your domain," like planting a garden, fixing the fence, putting in sprinklers, or coming up with a honey fix-it list if he's handy around the house and likes to tinker. Better yet, ask him what *he* would like to do. If he's home due to an illness or layoff, he especially needs to feel worthy, not worthless.

Remember, your husband lost space he called his own too, and if he's not welcome in his own home, he may turn to places and/or people who make him feel more at home.

GOD'S **LOVE LETTER** TO YOU

*Dear*_____,

"*Friends, this world is not your home, so don't make yourselves cozy in it. Don't indulge your ego at the expense of your soul*" (1 Peter 2:11 *The Message*).

The Head of Your Home, God

LET'S **PRAY**

Lord, help us adjust to this transition and remind us it might be as hard for our husbands as it is for us. We don't want to hold on too tightly to what we perceive as *ours*. This is *his* home too. We want to make our homes places of solace and refreshment. Give us patience, tolerance, empathy, and endurance. Amen.

The Magnet Syndrome

My retired husband is constantly coming up to me asking, "What are you doing?" He said he can't stay away—he's drawn to me like a magnet.

— MARIANN

Make room for the Master! Our Master Jesus has his arms wide open for you. — 1 CORINTHIANS 16:22–23 (*The Message*)

JANET'S JOURNAL

Dear God,

When we were first married, Dave literally followed me around the house wanting to do *everything* with me. He didn't have any friends or interests beside his job, golf, and me. We quickly remedied that dilemma by finding him friends, serving at church, and starting guitar lessons—the guitar eventually fell by the wayside.

Now I'm reliving those early years: it seems like every time I turn around, I'm running into him right behind me, or he's occupying the same space I'm trying to claim. I can't make a move without him showing up. I try having my "quiet time" outside, only to look up and see him coming out with his Bible ready to settle in across the table from me . . . which would be OK except he doesn't read *quietly* . . . he talks . . .

I get up early and go for my walk, expecting him to be done in the kitchen when I return. To my chagrin, he doesn't think about eating breakfast until I do! If I get my vitamins out of the cupboard, he needs his. Bottles fall and pills fly as we reach around each other trying to grab ours off the shelf.

When I go into the bathroom to put on my makeup and dry my hair, he remembers he needs to shave. Since we only have one sink and mirror, that's a big problem. Last night, I was trying to take a shower, and he had to go to the bathroom, even though he had just been in there flossing his teeth!

It's like having a perpetual shadow! Lord, I need some space. Why does everything I do trigger the exact same response in him? If I change my routine to accommodate him, he changes his routine to match mine—he's like a magnet. Help! I love my husband, but I'm stumbling over him at every turn.

Crowded, Janet

A WIFE SHARES: *Anita*

We were used to living in a seven-bedroom, 5000-square-foot home with a large kitchen. We retired in a downsized mountain home with small rooms, and my kitchen is one-fourth the size of the one in the bigger home. I'm petite and my husband, Gary, is a big guy, so it's difficult for us to be in the same space at the same time, which seems to happen all the time. I'm making my breakfast at the small kitchen counter, and there he comes to make his breakfast. If I have time, I'll just back away and go do something else until he's finished. I don't make a big deal about it.

But if we're both trying to get out of the house at the same time, we do a little dance around the kitchen trying to avoid bumping into each other or getting hit when one of us opens a cupboard, a drawer, or the refrigerator door.

MENTORING MOMENT

Anita shared the above story when we were walking together one morning and I was lamenting about what Dave and I now laughingly call the "magnet syndrome." Anita said she and Gary experience the same thing and then she shared the "breakfast dance" they often do in the mornings, just like Dave and me.

Anita also said she had been giving this phenomenon a lot of thought and concluded that the more time you spend together, the more you're on the same "wave length." You start thinking alike, your schedules are similar, and your body clocks become synchronized. You're both hungry simultaneously and sometimes even need to use the bathroom at the same time!

Then she pointed out this is how God intended marriage: husbands and wives become as one. When we each went our separate ways during the day, we had to transition back to being "one" when we saw each other again at night. Togetherness 24/7 reflects the oneness of Genesis 2:24—"For this reason a man will leave his father and mother and be united to his wife, and they will become one flesh."

Pondering Anita's words, I realized how right she was. Instead of operating as two separate people in a marriage, 24/7 husbands and wives truly transition into one body—spiritually and physically. Exactly what we all agreed to in our marriage vows when the pastor said, "I present to you Mr. and Mrs. _____ (fill in your names), united in marriage. What God has joined together, let no man separate."

GOD'S **LOVE LETTER** TO YOU

*Dear*_____,

Haven't you read that at the beginning I, the Creator, made you male and female, and said, "For this reason a man will leave his father and mother and be united to his wife, and the two will become one flesh." So you are no longer two, but one flesh. Therefore what I, God, have joined together, let no one separate (Matthew 19:4–6; paraphrased).

Your Magnet, God

LET'S **PRAY**

Lord, please help us not to feel, or express, that our husbands are in the way. Let us enjoy the experience of walking side-by-side on the same life path with them. Thank You for uniting us with our stay-at-home men in marriage and in life. Help us live as one with our husbands and celebrate our attraction to them physically, spiritually, and spatially. Instead of seeing the magnet syndrome as a burden, help us turn it into a blessing. Amen.

He's Home and I'm Not

I couldn't figure out how to be OK with me getting up and going to work and him staying home. — CHRIS

First thing in the morning, she dresses for work, rolls up her sleeves, eager to get started. She senses the worth of her work, is in no hurry to call it quits for the day. — PROVERBS 31:17–18 (*The Message*)

JANET'S **JOURNAL**

Dear God,

Our small mountain cabin in Idyllwild was my sanctuary . . . quiet, uninterrupted writing space. I'd go for a couple weeks . . . sometimes a month . . . and write continuously, while Dave stayed home and worked. I accomplished so much that when I came home, I could focus my time and energy on Dave, family, and friends.

This worked well until he had the reconstructive foot surgery and couldn't walk or drive for months, and I had to stay home with him while writing four books! Then we were back to "He's home and so am I, but I'm working and he's not!"

Missing my sanctuary, Janet

A WIFE **SHARES:** *Chris*

My husband, Pat, has been out of work several difficult times. It's hard for a man to feel his role as provider is undefined. Even more disheartening is when he applies over and over and nothing happens. The last time Pat was out of work was due to our country's economic struggles. It was a week after we buried my mom and we'd just checked into the hotel to celebrate our 38th wedding anniversary, when his boss called.

When Pat did find another job, it was entry-level, and the hours were terrible. He worked there a year before figuring out he could retire and make about the same amount he was making working long, hard, unpredictable hours. It was a no-brainer!

Now, if he'd retired the year before, I'm not sure I would have been ready. But after a very difficult year for both of us, no flexibility for even much of a social life, I was ready.

I have to say it has been fabulous. I'm married to a wonderful man who has always been willing to help when I asked. When he retired, he began picking up the slack at home while I still worked full time. We had agreed he would clean house so we could save money. He also began washing clothes, running errands, emptying the dishwasher, and other "honey-dos." I no longer have to run errands after work or on the weekends. He even gets dinner started before I get home and helps me finish up and clean up.

I'm careful to notice what he does and to tell him daily how much I appreciate him. If I'd known how wonderful his retirement was going to be, I think I would have been ready earlier! Truly, though, this was God's timing and He had prepared both Pat and me for this next step in our journey.

MENTORING MOMENT

When I told a friend with a retired husband that I was writing *Dear God, He's Home!*, before I could say the subtitle . . . she barbed, "And I'm not!" A working wife, or a wife who has had to go to work, may feel the burden of supporting the family when she'd rather be home.

An article in *Time* magazine, "Life After Work" by Sharon Epperson, discusses the battle couples go through deciding what each will do in retirement and who will retire first. Epperson quotes Jon Skillman, president of Fidelity Investments Life Insurance Co.: "Married couples can be relatively in synch with one another when it comes to making decisions about how they want to live today—where to go to dinner or where to take the next family vacation. Yet surprisingly, husband and wives do not necessarily see eye to eye on their expectations for retirement."

When a stay-at-home man takes over household chores while the wife continues working, she's blessed. However, not all husbands are willing or capable of helping around the house. More often wives complain that when they walk in the door from work, their husbands are sitting on the couch asking what's for dinner. Or she still has to come home and take care of a sick or disabled husband plus all the household chores. Just like a wife with a deployed husband, her work doubles, and it's hard not to become resentful and exhausted.

If you didn't get to retire first or had to go back to work, or you're holding down the household during his deployment, illness, or disability, don't be afraid to propose ideas for lightening your workload at home. It's better to unveil your frustrations and angry feelings, than letting negative emotions simmer and percolate in your heart until they spew out with words you can't control or take back.

Start all discussions with prayer. Share how you're feeling with your husband without using the accusatory *you* or all-inclusive words like *never* or *always*. Be watchful of not comparing him with other husbands in your thoughts or words. Comparing won't motivate your husband, but it will alienate him. It's a lose-lose manipulative tactic sure to close your husband's spirit and ears.

GOD'S LOVE LETTER TO YOU

*Dear*_____,

Be joyful always; pray continually; give thanks in all circumstances, for this is My will for you in Christ Jesus (1 Thessalonians 5:16–18 NLT; paraphrased).

Your Mediator, God

LET'S **PRAY**

Father, it just doesn't seem fair. We don't want to be in this position and, yet, we know we should be content in all circumstances because our hope is in You. Our peace is in You, Lord. Thank You, Jesus! Amen.

YOUR LETTER TO GOD

A "new normal" transition time is difficult. How are you coping with the unexpected changes? How is your marriage doing? How can God help?

Dear God,   *Date:*

_____

_____

_____

_____

_____

_____

_____

_____

FOR **DISCUSSION**

1. How are your husband and you different? Do you *balance* or *blame* each other? Explain:

2. Describe any "space" issues and solutions.

3. How do you experience the magnet syndrome? Can you laugh about it or is it still a source of contention?

Chapter 5:
DEALING WITH REACTIONS

People ask Alan if he likes retirement, does he have enough to do to keep busy. He always answers in the affirmative. I believe he's making up for lost time. He has established routines, never misses his quiet time, listens to all his iPod downloads in a timely fashion, keeps abreast in the political arena, soaks up history and the constitution, reads, and stays generally informed. — NANCY

Words kill, words give life; they're either poison or fruit—you choose. — PROVERBS 18:21 (*The Message*)

Telling the Family

What really blessed us early on was the response we got from each of our four kids when Ken was laid off. — DEBORAH

Families stick together in all kinds of trouble. — PROVERBS 17:17 (*The Message*)

JANET'S JOURNAL

Dear God,

When Dave lost his job the first time, I had just resigned my career to go into full-time lay ministry and writing. With both of us home and out of work, our family thought we had "lost it" and I should find a job quickly. Lord, You were using me to launch Woman to Woman Mentoring at Saddleback Church, and I *was* working—for You. This was hard for the kids to understand. They asked me, "What are you doing up there in the office all the time?" when I was hard at work writing the Woman to Woman Mentoring resources to help other churches start their own mentoring ministries.

Daughter Kim fretted over what to tell people when they asked what her parents were doing: "They're both out of work and my mom, who has never written anything in her life, wants to become an author!" She continually asked if the church was paying me. Kim wasn't a believer yet and didn't understand we couldn't put a dollar value on the lives we saw changing in the Mentoring Ministry.

About His Work, Janet

A WIFE **SHARES:** *Deborah*

We moved to New York as newlyweds and had a "poverty" adventure living on oatmeal for one week. We'd told our kids this story many times in the context of, "If you have to choose one food to live on three meals a day, oatmeal is a good one (even though we were *sick* of oatmeal).

After calling our kids to tell them about Ken's layoff, a package arrived from our oldest daughter. We opened it to find a box of Quaker oats! Just the reminder we needed of God's promise to provide, and such a blessing to realize our kids had listened to our stories of God's provisions and were praying and trusting Him for us!

MENTORING MOMENT

Children often perceive parents as invincible providers capable of overcoming any obstacle. It's unnerving when we appear vulnerable or struggling, but it's also healthy for the family to see how Christians handle life's inevitable transitions and crises. Do we react like much of the world by drinking too much, doing drugs, falling into depression, giving up, getting a divorce . . . ? Or do we show our children an example of trusting and relying on God? It shouldn't be a hard choice.

It's easy to trust God when everything is going great, but when trials and hardships beset us, our family should see that we live out what we *say* we believe. They're going to have difficulties too—everyone does—and we need to be their role models for challenging times.

GOD'S **LOVE LETTER** TO YOU

*Dear*_____,

Even if your father and mother abandon you, I the LORD *will hold you close* (Psalm 27:10 NLT; paraphrased).

Your Heavenly Father, God

LET'S **PRAY**

Lord, it's so difficult to see the fear in our family's eyes. They're wondering how we're going to make it, and sometimes we wonder too. But we're confident that You're going before us, preparing the way. Give us words to encourage and assure our loved ones You will never leave or forsake us . . . or them. Let our actions mentor the family in how to go through their own unexpected or transitional times. Help us be a witness to Your faithfulness. Amen.

People Say the Darnedest Things

"I used to be a . . . " The words make me self-conscious as I wonder if the person is thinking, *Why aren't you still doing that now?* — CHERI

I found myself in trouble and went looking for my Lord; my life was an open wound that wouldn't heal. When friends said, "Everything will turn out all right," I didn't believe a word they said. — PSALM 77:2 (*The Message*)

JANET'S **JOURNAL**

Dear God,

When Dave was out of work from layoffs, it was hard recounting the story of what happened and why he couldn't find a job. There were many unsolicited suggestions—do this or try that. He even found himself unsuspectingly attending multilevel marketing meetings. His self-worth and self-esteem were already assaulted, and peoples' condescending comments or asking, "What are you going to do?" didn't help.

Then when he lost his job due to his foot surgery, it seemed everyone had an opinion of what we should do next. When all we really needed to hear was, "I'm praying for you. In fact, let's pray right now for wisdom and discernment."

When he later retired, he fended off, "What do you do all day?"

Exasperated, Janet

A STAY-AT-HOME MAN **SHARES:** *Joseph*

When diagnosed with Agent Orange and my wife left our three kids and me, I was an aging marine warrior washing and folding clothes, supervising baths, and packing lunches. Add mopping the floor and making dinner to the list. Oh yes, did I mention helping with homework?

My first thought was to find a woman to help me. Isn't that what men are supposed to do when the kids are 10, 7, and 5? I joined the Web site Match.com in search of an easier life, with romance a decidedly secondary and hidden motive. Match.com promises one out of five marriages originate on the Internet. Aah . . . my answers were just a click of my computer's mouse away!

I wrote 235 women within a 100-mile radius of my house. During a six-week period, I had two dates. The others said I had one kid too many. Or I was a tad grizzly in my profile picture. Oh sure, there were those who admired a man who would raise three kids, but they couldn't quite pull the trigger. Maybe I was nuts to even try.

MENTORING MOMENT

Cheri in the opening quote said she hoped her former colleague was correct when he advised: "People don't think about you as much as you think about you!" He was right-on. People can seem insensitive, patronizing, condescending . . . even hurtful . . . but they're just not thinking!

They may offer a cliché or something that minimizes your situation because people are innately uncomfortable around someone suffering. Trudy said she and her husband stopped saying "out of work" and changed their response to "retired."

At times, you too may be the insensitive person saying the wrong thing and in need of forgiveness. God reminds us how to communicate with each other: "*Well-spoken words bring satisfaction*" (Proverbs 12:14 *The Message*).

Nonsatirical humor often defrays uncomfortable situations, but your goal isn't to offend or embarrass the person. Don't respond sarcastically, defensively, or angrily. Instead, *"[speak] the truth in love"* (Ephesians 4:15).

GOD'S **LOVE LETTER** TO YOU

*Dear*_____,

You must make allowance for each other's faults and forgive the person who offends you. Remember, I forgave you, so you must forgive others. And the most important piece of clothing you must wear is love. Love is what binds us all together in perfect harmony. And let the peace that comes from My Son, Jesus Christ, rule in your hearts. For as members of one body you are all called to live in peace. And always be thankful (Colossians 3:13–15 NLT; paraphrased).

Peacefully, God

LET'S **PRAY**

Lord, You know the things people say that cut to the core. It makes us angry and often we want to lash back or avoid them completely. Help us respond in love and not receive into our hearts anything not spoken in love. Lord, please guard our own mouths when we're tempted to say the wrong thing at the wrong time. Help us forgive those who hurt us as You have forgiven us. Amen.

He Said, She Said

Throughout our deployment and reintegration, I will strive to remain tender and broken before Christ, so I can be prepared to forgive with a "forgiving love." — SHERRY

I pray every morning for patience and not to be cranky with my husband. — MICHELLE

The biggest challenge has been forgiving my ex-wife. It's a struggle not to let bitterness consume me. — JOSEPH

Kind words heal and help; cutting words wound and maim.
— PROVERBS 15:4 (*The Message*)

JANET'S JOURNAL

Dear God,

It's seems like we're fighting all the time now that Dave's home. We seldom quarreled before—maybe because we spent the majority of the day apart and now we spend most of our time together in a new situation with different parameters.

We definitely don't know how to fight fair. We're slinging out words and threats that never passed our lips before. We seem continually irritated at each other and neither of us can do anything right in the other's eyes. I think he says something different than he meant and vice versa. Sometimes it feels like the *War of the Roses* . . . well maybe not that bad . . . but we don't want to spend the rest of our lives this way. Help!

I'm sure it's just the stress of navigating a new season of life. Lord, I've written about how to resolve conflict—please help me apply it in my own life.

Struggling, Janet

A WIFE SHARES: *Mona*

Why couldn't we get along? Everything we said and heard had the sting of a piercing sniper aiming to take each other out. Not realizing the pain each hit was causing, the firing continued.

Nineteen years had flown by since we vowed to become one and our love was so respectful, endearing, promising, and seemingly impenetrable. We were partners in everything and assisted each other in developing two businesses. We trusted each other.

Now we were functioning professionally, yet dying personally and intimately. The last two years had been an emotional desert between us. The integrity of our marriage was in jeopardy!

Then while on a business trip I received the unforgettable text, *"Have we wasted nearly 20 years of life together?"*

My answer, an absolute, *"No!"*

Yet he had discovered emails between a male business acquaintance and me during this vulnerable time. Neither of us realized the problem—lost communication.

Texts flew back and forth in cyberspace. The electronic communication broke the silence by keeping the messages direct, concise, and to the point. Painful truths filled with anger. This could become an obstacle violating our journey as life partners.

The pain of repentance surpassed physical pain, but God, the Almighty Physician, pulled both hearts back into one. I believe in a forgiving God who washes, cleanses, and renews. We begged God to go back to work continuing what He had begun in us. Our distractions ceased with the supernatural power to change and our decision to hear and obey God's voice through His Word.

From that time of emotional pain, until we reach eternity, there is nothing better than to hear and see my beloved husband come home!

MENTORING MOMENT

I saw what could easily become Dave and me as I observed an elderly couple behind me in line at the grocery store. "I said put the *cold* things together, Frank!" the wife hissed at her husband as she deliberately rearranged the items he had just placed on the checkout belt. "I did . . . " he said resignedly as a defeated look conveyed, *I can't do anything right by her.*

Elaine W. Miller asks in *We All Married Idiots*, "How many of us make wrong choices when our loved ones err? We steam over stupid stuff. Let go and enjoy your marriage—with and without the mistakes. . . . Finding the humor in an error of judgment can help heal the humiliation."

On her *Faith Deployed* blog—faithdeployed.com—Jocelyn Green interviewed author and psychologist Dr. Gary Rosberg and Barb Rosberg of America's Family Coaches. The topic was reintegration for military families, but the Rosbergs' suggestions and tips can apply to couples going through the process of adjusting to a stay-at-home man for any reason:

1. Affirm before your spouse, your family, and your Lord that we will not even utter the word *divorce.*
2. Press into each other and Jesus during your "reintegration," forging a relationship of three by praying together.
3. Connect to each other. Grab a few minutes, a couple of chairs, face each other, turn off anything that plugs in or runs on a battery (all technology), and give each other your undivided attention for up to 20 minutes daily.

4. Boundary up! Guard love. They quote Dr. Howard Hendricks at Dallas Theological Seminary: "The enemy will lie in wait for 40 years to find the weak spot in the armor of a man" (or woman). You have the power of the Holy Spirit to resist—use it.
5. Be the first to forgive. Keep your heart tender and broken before Christ.

Number 5 deserves elaboration because it's a key factor in resolving conflict. Here is a paraphrase of the Rosbergs' wise counsel:

> Be the first one to forgive, to release your spouse for whatever it is that the enemy is allowing to be empowered to kill your marriage and harden your heart . . . a hard heart precedes isolation, withdrawal, toxic emotions, and breakdown of the walls protecting your marriage. What is the antidote? Let go. Surrender. Forgive. . . . Love your spouse the way Christ loves them. Unconditionally. Without reservation. Are there consequences to offenses? Yes. Do they take time to heal? Yes. But when you choose to love again, when you choose to be like Jesus with skin on, when you choose to forgive, you set a prisoner free to learn you have been the prisoner (Lewis Smedes's great insight).

Consider studying with your spouse, or in a group, my Bible study, *Face-to-Face with Euodia and Syntyche: From Conflict to Community.* It includes "7 Steps to Biblically Resolving Conflict," which are also in "Sanity Tools," page 182.

GOD'S **LOVE LETTER** TO YOU

*Dear*_____,

Forgive your brothers and sisters and spouses from your heart (Matthew 18:35 NLT; paraphrased). *"Above all else, guard your heart, for it is the wellspring of life"* (Proverbs 4:23).

Continually Forgiving, God

LET'S **PRAY**

Oh Lord, we know how Satan uses our pride and the desire to be right to infuse conflict into our marriage relationship. When we haven't seen our husbands for a while, or we've seen them too much for a long while, our hearts can grow hard toward them and our mouths reveal what's in our hearts. We can't take back misspoken words. Help us guard our hearts, minds, actions, and words and to be the first to forgive and reconcile. With Your help, we can, and will, do this. Amen.

YOUR LETTER TO GOD

Who do you need to ask for forgiveness or to forgive? Write his or her name in your journal entry here and pray for the right time and place. Forgiveness frees you from the burden of bitterness getting a foothold in your mind and heart.

Dear God,   *Date:*

_____

_____

_____

_____

_____

_____

_____

_____

_____

_____

_____

_____

_____

_____

_____

_____

_____

_____

_____

FOR **DISCUSSION**

1. How did family respond to your stay-at-home man transition and how did that make you feel?

2. What is your typical reaction to "unthinking" comments? List possible loving and kind responses:

3. Rate yourself on the Rosbergs' five tips for "reintegrating" your husband, regardless of the reason he's home. How can you improve in each area?

Chapter 6:

GETTING NEEDED SUPPORT

I'm so grateful Jerry was working from home when we cared for my mother in our home for two and a half years before she passed away. His prayerful support and physical presence helped me maintain a godly perspective on the caregiving process. He was my sounding board and relief team. With the help of God and my dear husband, I was able to spend quality time with my mother during her last days. I am forever grateful to him for his sacrificial love for both Mom and me. — DEBBIE

All praise to the God and Father of our Master, Jesus the Messiah! Father of all mercy! God of all healing counsel! He comes alongside us when we go through hard times, and before you know it, he brings us alongside someone else who is going through hard times so that we can be there for that person just as God was there for us.

— 2 CORINTHIANS 1:3–4 (*The Message*)

We Need Help

My kids go to a Christian school and some of the teachers have stepped up to help. — JOSEPH

So how should I prepare to come to you? As a severe disciplinarian who makes you toe the mark? Or as a good friend and counselor who wants to share heart-to-heart with you? You decide.

— 1 CORINTHIANS 4:21 (*The Message*)

JANET'S JOURNAL

Dear God,

For years, every Monday morning Dave got up and met his friend John at 6:00 A.M. They saw each other through health, family, and job issues and celebrated good times together. Dave never told me what they talked about; I didn't ask.

Dave now gets up early on Thursday mornings to go to our church men's group and then they all go to breakfast and talk some more. I'm grateful Dave recognizes there are some things only another man understands, like I often need to talk to another woman. Dave always seems in better spirits when he returns home.

Encouraged, Janet

A WIFE SHARES: *Nancy*

When the radiologist confirmed bilateral pulmonary emboli, Alan thought, *death*. I saw fear in his eyes. The good news: He survived. We spent Christmas in ICU and the remainder of the week in the hospital, but went home New Year's Eve expecting a full recovery and to get back to work.

Unfortunately, tests showed deep venous thrombosis in his legs, previously asymptomatic. After surgery, recovery was slow and the thought of disability was a looming threat to my dedicated doctor husband.

A few months later, our daughter's alcoholic husband lost his job and disappeared, leaving her alone with a 14-month-old, which added to Alan's anxiety. Realizing he needed help, Alan sought counseling for himself and was diagnosed with, and treated for, PTSD.

MENTORING MOMENT

Men often feel uncomfortable—even shameful—getting professional help. They've been accustomed to "handling" their career and home life and fear admitting—especially to each other—that they can't handle things any longer will make them appear less of a man. Soldiers often arrive home with varying degrees of PTSD or injuries, but as Nancy's story above reveals, men don't have to go to war to suffer some of the same symptoms.

Life is hard and most of us will encounter trauma, disappointments, grief, fear. . . . We need to encourage our husbands and ourselves to let others step in and help us during difficult times, and sometimes that means professional help. We'll talk in the next session about finding someone who can understand or has been in your shoes, but for now be sure the person you're talking to is a Christian who shares your views and values.

The first step in regaining our peace is admitting we need help; the second is locating the safest and most effective place to obtain help; the third is stepping out to help someone else.

GOD'S **LOVE LETTER** TO YOU

*Dear*_____,

For you a child was born, to you a son is given, and the government will be on his shoulders. And he will be called Wonderful Counselor, Mighty God, Everlasting Father, Prince of Peace (Isaiah 9:6; paraphrased).

Your Counselor, God

LET'S **PRAY**

Lord, it's humbling to admit we need help. It makes us feel so needy and weak. Help us remember that when we are weak, You are strong enough for both of us. Amen.

Joining or Starting a Support Group

I'm too private to do a support group, but an 80-ish lady at church helped me, and I've talked to another friend whose husband is home.

— PRISCILLA

If you think you know it all, you're a fool for sure; real survivors learn wisdom from others. — PROVERBS 28:26 (*The Message*)

JANET'S **JOURNAL**

Dear God,

I don't know how we would have made it through all the transitions in our life without the support of our small group and friends. Just knowing they cared about us and were praying for us lifted our spirits. Going to small group Bible study gave Dave an opportunity to get out of the house and enjoy a change of pace.

Studying Your Word with fellow believers brought us back to the Source of our hope and joy—You! We could also be a witness of Your faithfulness as we went through our various trials and transitions. Over the years, many of our friends experienced layoffs and setbacks, and they always knew they could talk to us.

During Dave's layoffs, he also attended a group at church focused on helping people find work. There was comfort in being around others going through something similar and knowing he was not alone.

Supportively, Janet

A WIFE SHARES: *Nancy*

Alan has joined an online Campus Crusade Ministry/Global Media Outreach that replies to spiritual commitments and questions from around the world. He can do this from his computer any day, every day.

I've been involved with Women's Ministry for many years with our daytime Bible studies. I can participate when home and use my computer when traveling. I'm part of the team writing our daily online devotionals, which are easy to do when I'm away. I've been able to co-facilitate a small-group Bible study and only missed two weeks.

MENTORING MOMENT

Like the men and women sharing in this book, others in your vicinity are experiencing what you're going through. Forming a group together creates a safe place to share your doubts and fears, your hopes and ideas. Electronics make it possible to participate in virtual groups if you can't physically go to a group or you're traveling.

If your husband is home due to illness or disability, you've likely become a caregiver and many churches and medical facilities offer support groups specifically for caregivers. Give yourself a break and hire a sitter if you have to, but join a group where you feel comfortable and welcome. It helps being around others who understand your world. I endorsed a book two of my author friends co-wrote, *JOY-spirations for Caregivers* (see p. 178), and I highly recommend this walk-along-beside-you devotional.

Likewise, if you're a military wife, your support needs are unique. Joining with other military wives provides a sense of community when you're feeling isolated and alone. There are also online support group blogs you can join right from your home. One I recommend is Jocelyn Green's faithdeployed.com. For more ideas on retreats and conferences for military marriages, see page 178 in "Sanity Tools."

Alice said her adult kids and her older sister, who had already transitioned into having a stay-at-home husband, functioned as her "support group" when her husband retired. Often family members, and your church family, can provide much needed mentoring and encouragement.

Many of the core issues involving a stay-at-home man are similar, regardless of the situation bringing him home. On page 188, you'll find a small-group guide to help form a support group of wives with stay-at-home husbands or a couples' group. The group isn't a gripe session, but a place to share ideas and pick up tips from others. It's also an opportunity to pray and fellowship together.

A support group won't be a panacea, but every journey is more enjoyable and tolerable accompanied by someone who knows the territory. Maybe God is calling you to start such a group—something to pray about.

GOD'S LOVE LETTER TO YOU

Dear_____,

Don't give up meeting together, as some are in the habit of doing, but encourage one another—and all the more as you see the Day approaching (Hebrews 10:25; paraphrased).

Supportively, God

LET'S PRAY

God, please help us reach out to others who understand our situation. Everything is so personal, and yet we know we could benefit from spending time with wives and couples who share our experiences. Help us be givers and not just takers of understanding and compassion. Provide our husbands and us with someone we feel comfortable talking to, and perhaps we can form new friendships. Guide us to the group You know is best for us, or if it's Your plan, provide us stamina and courage to start a group ourselves. Amen.

Others Have Survived This — We Will Too

I'm praying for you and your family going through this layoff. Believe me when I say I know exactly how numb, sad, and scared you feel. I can't promise it will be easy, but I *can* promise God will be there with you every step of the way.

— DEBORAH (to another wife whose husband lost his job)

As iron sharpens iron, so one man sharpens another.

— PROVERBS 27:17

JANET'S JOURNAL

Dear God,

I'm a passionate proponent of people sharing their life's experiences to help others. So many times in the Woman to Woman Mentoring Ministry, or at conferences and retreats, I've heard women lament about husbands losing jobs, disabled, ill, or retiring and the ensuing difficulties. I listened with a sympathetic ear but couldn't visualize this ever happening to us.

Lord, are You using our many transitions to foster more empathy and compassion in me? Do you want me to reach out from my own experiences to help someone even when I don't have things figured out myself? I know it only takes a willing and loving heart. Sometimes others just need a hug and listening ear—it's always helped me. I can do that!

Surviving and thriving, Janet

A WIFE SHARES: *Pam*

Pam Farrel's husband, Bill, now works out of their home. The following paraphrased excerpt from Pam's book *52 Ways to Wow Your Husband*, is an example of how another woman's experience and perspective can mentor us, even about coffee cups:

My husband, Bill, loves his coffee. But along with Bill's love of coffee, he also has a habit that could be very annoying, that is his aversion to get the coffee mugs into the dishwasher. I find coffee cups every place imaginable: in the garage, in the car, in the truck, in the closet, on the sidewalk, on the deck and patio, in

70

the shop, in the office, on the stairwell, in the bathroom—you name it, and I have likely found a coffee cup there.

One day, as we were preparing to move homes, I was doing that "last load of dishes" and I realized it was composed of all coffee mugs! Forty-seven of them to be exact! It made me smile because years ago I decided to pray for Bill every time I saw one of his empty displaced mugs. I was seeking to apply the principle *"Love covers over a multitude of sins"* (1 Peter 4:8).

I have embraced the ever reappearing dirty coffee mug with fond affection because it reminds me of my hardworkin' man who requires caffeine to do all the wonderful acts of service that benefit so many—including me.

MENTORING MOMENT

As you've read in this book, I often use my own—or someone else's—story to encourage and help others going through something similar. You may think you can't reach out to someone until you've resolved your own issues, but helping leads to healing—them and you. Many of the quotes from Sharing Wife Deborah, whose husband Ken went through a layoff, came from an email she sent to a girlfriend whose husband had also lost his job.

God doesn't give us character-building experiences solely for our own benefit. He wants us using the many ways we've seen Him work in our life to encourage and mentor someone going through something similar. We're to share the "been-there-done-that" experiences God helps us through to assure others that God will help them too, and so will we.

I paraphrase the foundation passage for Woman to Woman Mentoring, Titus 2:3–5: Teach what you've been taught so you can train others to teach what you've taught them. Mentoring is simply sharing life's lessons with others.

GOD'S LOVE LETTER TO YOU

*Dear*_____,

"I, God, am able to make all grace abound to you, so that in all things at all times, having all that you need, you will abound in every good work" (2 Corinthians 9:8; paraphrased).

Your Mentor, God

LET'S **PRAY**

Heavenly Mentor, we don't want to impose on others, but this is all so new to us. Please bring someone to share with us the wisdom You've given her. Help us remain humble and willing to listen and learn. Lord, please remind us to pass on to others what You teach us. Amen.

YOUR LETTER TO GOD

Thank God for each source of encouragement and support and ask Him to show you who needs your encouragement and support.

Dear God,   *Date:*

_____

_____

_____

_____

_____

_____

_____

FOR **DISCUSSION**

1. What is the value of a support or small group?

2. Why does it help to know that others have survived something similar?

3. Where could you find a mentor? Who could you mentor from your experiences?

Chapter 7:

MAKING IT THROUGH
THE BAD DAYS

We've all experienced the strain of emotional disconnect on our marriages—whether through predeployment, deployment, reintegration, or even the everyday routines of life. Often it's easier to see this disconnect in our husbands, commonly referred to as a glorified "survival technique." But let's face it . . . we struggle with this too! The multiple separations take their toll on the best of us, and we find ourselves struggling with disappointments, discouragements, distance, disconnect, discord, and even emotional divorce. — SHERRY

If God hadn't been there for me, I never would have made it.
The minute I said, "I'm slipping, I'm falling,"
your love, GOD, took hold and held me fast.
When I was upset and beside myself,
you calmed me down and cheered me up.
— PSALM 94:17–19 (*The Message*)

God's Waiting Room

While waiting for an interview process to unfold for Richard, I paraphrased and wrote several verses from Isaiah 65 on a piece of paper I kept in my pocket. When the waiting became too stressful, I'd read them. Just touching the paper brought comfort and I felt God's closeness. We continued to pray and wait and wait and pray. — CHAR

Be still before the Lord and wait patiently for him. —PSALM 37:7

JANET'S JOURNAL

Dear God,

Dave and I didn't wait long to get married—only six months of dating—but we've languished in many of Your waiting rooms. We waited 18 long stressful months for Dave to find a job after his first layoff. Four years later, we waited for my disappointing breast cancer biopsy results and for Dave to find another job after a second layoff.

Thinking I was cancer-free after six years, we were surprised to be waiting again for biopsy results, which revealed I had a recurrence.

After Dave's reconstructive foot surgery, we watched and waited for his foot to heal so he could go back to work. Not the answer we wanted there either—he lost his job when recovery took a year instead of the six months the company allowed.

Then we waited for our house to sell so we could move to a state with a lower cost of living and we waited to find the right house when we decided on Idaho. Then we waited for the big traumatic move.

It was great having Dave home to help prepare for leaving our home of 23 years, but we waited to get into a workable routine and not clash at every turn.

When we finally settled in our new home and state, we waited a third time for biopsy results that were again . . . disappointing.

Do You use all our waiting times to draw us closer to You and to each other? Lord, is there still more waiting to come?

Impatiently waiting, Janet

A WIFE SHARES: *Beth*

It's not retirement time for my husband. Until now, he's always been employed accept when he was either healing from a surgery due to recreational activities or occasionally off work for back problems. Now, it's a different season—no job.

We've been married for 34 years, but we couldn't retire if we wanted to. We're in a hurry-up-and-wait circumstance after a declining economy resulted in us losing everything we had gained financially over the past 15 years.

We're back on track, but it's slow. So what I realize the most is I must trust the Lord and accept that He has allowed this to occur in our lives. Income and busyness previously masked many things surfacing now.

Our whole routine has changed, and I'm pretty sure it's going to change again, so I wait to make some adjustments I should make right away—like continue going to Bible study, fellowshipping, and most of all, staying in the Word.

MENTORING MOMENT

I've been impatient my entire life. Even though I try to practice patience, I often fail. Waiting can make us tense and irritable—it does me. Maintaining a normal schedule is my waiting survival technique. I wait best staying busy. Carrying on as usual leaves little time to dwell on the circumstances or worry about the future.

It's nerve-racking when daily life is drastically—possibly permanently—disrupted by your husband coming home . . . maybe forever . . . and maybe different than he was before. It consumes your thoughts. Returning to *normal* activities, when you wonder if life will ever be *normal* again, may seem impossible. Let me assure you, it's the best therapy. While we can never go back to the days before our husbands came home—whether willingly or forced—we can maximize each new day the Lord gives us.

Our family and friends will also cope better if they see us doing the things we did before. Waiting periods allow everyone to adjust to potential change. For now, live one day at a time. This isn't denial: It's living in the present.

GOD'S LOVE LETTER TO YOU

Dear_____,

I, the Lord, long to be gracious to you; I rise to show you compassion. For I, the Lord, am a God of justice. Blessed are all who wait for Me! (Isaiah 30:18; paraphrased).

Waiting with You, God

LET'S PRAY

We waited patiently for You, Lord; You turned to us and heard our cry. You lifted us out of the slimy pit, out of the mud and mire; you set our feet on a rock and gave us a firm place to stand. You put a new song in our mouth, a hymn of praise to our God. Many will see and fear and put their trust in You, Lord. Amen.

—PSALM 40:1–3 (PARAPHRASED AND PERSONALIZED)

Anxious Days and Sleepless Nights

After Ken's layoff, I'd wake up in the night trembling with fear and sneak out of bed to sit by the fireplace with my Bible. I'd read and read until finally peace came . . . and it always did . . . at least enough for that night. — DEBORAH

I go to bed and think, "How long till I can get up?" I toss and turn as the night drags on—and I'm fed up! —JOB 7:4 (*The Message*)

JANET'S JOURNAL

Dear God,

We've been talking for several years about moving out of Southern California, but the main problem was finding a job for Dave with health benefits, since I was uninsurable with my breast cancer recurrences. Now that Dave can't work and is retiring on disability, and we learned that I can go on COBRA until I'm eligible for Medicare, a new window of opportunity has opened and we've started looking for a place in Idaho near daughter Kim's family and three of our grandchildren.

It's a huge step for us, but when our house sold, we knew it was You, Lord, giving us the go-ahead, but still I look at this move with anxiety and anticipation . . . mainly anxiety.

Retiring and moving—two major life transitions at once! What if we hate Idaho or can't make it financially? What if being together 24/7 drives us crazy? Can I talk Dave into finding a part-time job? Will we make new friends? What about finding a church? I've *never* lived far from the ocean. Will it be too hot . . . too cold . . . snowbound in the winter? If Dave can't walk well, how will he do with ice and snow?

What will we do with all our furniture? What should we take and what should we sell? Can we get everything done in the month we now have to pack and vacate our home? We're fighting over everything—even what boxes to use and where to buy them. I'm exhausted at night, but my mind won't stop racing. Are we crazy? Can our marriage survive so many changes at once? Only You, Lord, hold the answers, and what do I gain by worrying? Lost sleep, that's what . . .

Sleepless in Orange County, Janet

A WIFE **SHARES:** *Char*

In 2008, the economy tanked. Supportive friends told us it usually took three months after a layoff to find a professional position. As three months stretched into a year and Richard attended one networking meeting after another, we realized there was no quick fix to our situation.

Unemployment benefits expired—we began drawing down our savings. COBRA expired—we began paying for private health insurance. Vision and dental coverage expired—we skipped our annual exams.

"Dear God, please show me You're at work in our situation," I begged as things seemingly got worse. I didn't think I could handle the anxiety over a prolonged job search.

MENTORING MOMENT

Every night at 3:00 A.M., I'd wake up tossing and turning. It was so frustrating until, like Deborah in the opening quote, I decided to stop fighting it and get up. I remembered King David wrote to God in Psalm 17:3 (*The Message*), "*Go ahead, examine me from inside out, surprise me in the middle of the night.*" Then awake in Psalm 63:6 (*The Message*), David spent the time thinking back on good things: "*If I'm sleepless at midnight, I spend the hours in grateful reflection.*"

Another psalmist used the night hours to thank God: "*I get up in the middle of the night to thank you; your decisions are so right, so true—I can't wait till morning!*" (Psalm 119:62 *The Message*).

Deborah and I found the middle of the night an excellent time to talk to God—maybe praying or reading the Bible will comfort you back to sleep too. I do know that getting angry and frustrated with insomnia, or the fact that your husband is sleeping soundly, doesn't help.

Try the following practical tips:

- Avoid caffeine, sugar, and chocolate in the evening.
- Sip herbal "sleepy-time" or caffeine-free tea before bedtime.
- Don't watch the late news; it'll keep you up for sure.
- Turn off television at least one hour before bedtime. Television stimulates the brain. You might fall asleep, but may have bad dreams or wake up later in the night.
- My favorite—talk your husband into giving you a relaxing backrub with an aromatherapy oil or lotion or give one to him.

- Take a warm—not too hot—bath or shower.
- Read comforting Scriptures.
- Journal to God in this book. Get it all out of your mind and onto paper.
- Say a nighttime prayer together asking God for nourishing, comforting, essential sleep.
- A great Scripture to pray is the one below under "Let's Pray" . . . especially the last sentence.

GOD'S **LOVE LETTER** TO YOU

Dear_____,

"My Presence will go with you, and I will give you rest" (Exodus 33:14).

Reassuring, God

LET'S **PRAY**

Prayerfully Personalize Psalm 3:4–5 and 4:8 (NLT):
Lord, I'm weary and tired and I need Your help . . . .
I _____ cried out to the Lord, and he answered me from his holy mountain. I _____ lay down and slept. I _____ woke up in safety, for the Lord was watching over me. I _____ will lie down in peace and sleep, for you alone, Oh Lord, will keep me safe. Amen.

The Journey Can Be Lonely

My husband just got back from active duty two months ago. We're just past the "honeymoon" stage, and it's HARD. Maybe not so much for him (he makes it look like he's adjusting just fine, thank you very much). I'm feeling disconnected, and he's adjusting to a new command.

— LAURA

I wasn't only alone, but sick and home alone with three children under ten.

— JOSEPH

Turn to me and have mercy on me, because I am lonely and hurting.

— PSALM 25:16 (NCV)

JANET'S JOURNAL

Dear God,

A move to Idaho in our 60s is a huge deal! People look at us in one of two ways: admiringly because we're doing what they've always wanted to do, or skeptically because we have no idea what we're doing. I vacillate between those two extremes myself.

Like Abraham and Sarah in the Bible, we are literally packing up and going into the unknown—alone. Leaving behind a comfortable life—a home where I've lived for 23 years and we raised our children; doctors, friends, daughter Shannon's family with two of our grandchildren, favorite stores, Saddleback Church where we met and served . . . and the weather I love—the known. And going to live in a mountain community with four definite seasons and very few amenities, where we know no one, don't have a church or friends, and our daughter Kim's family lives over an hour away. . . . What are we doing?

Lonely, Janet

TWO WIVES SHARE: *Sherry*

Throughout our brief reintegration, knowing another deployment is two weeks away, we strain and struggle to share painful feelings we'd like to bury, or better yet, have vanish. Although we pray for one another and spend time pondering God's Word, we haven't taken time to pray together or sit down face-to-face and talk heart-to-heart.

I strive to verbalize my emotions: "I feel . . ." or "I will cherish . . ." My husband keeps silent, not knowing what to say. His nonresponse fuels my emotional distance. I often struggle to feel the same closeness, connection, and intimacy we once had.

I long for past memories of time spent together in prayer. I continue to look for ways to connect, to meet his needs and encourage him; but knowing our time is so limited, I bring my deepest heart longings to the Lord to carry for me.

I'm grateful to serve a living God who knows and understands my every struggle and need. I cling to the truth, knowing the intimacy with my husband is there, clouded by overwhelming emotions as deployment is upon us. We will guard our love by pressing into each other and Jesus.

May the Lord show me how to reconnect through the reintegration process, to build a lasting love and experience our dream marriage.

Amy

It's hard being alone when they're gone, but also difficult, and some-times puzzling, when they're physically home but still intensely process-ing their recent war experiences—outside the realm of "normal." When my husband returned home from a traumatic deployment, it seemed like he didn't carry on a conversation with me for several months. He just said war changes everyone. It was hard not to take the silence for rejection.

He loves his precious Lord, Jesus Christ, but nagging him into talking and praying with me wouldn't work. Unconditional love, patience, and maintaining my relationship with God are the keys to getting through a time of disconnect.

MENTORING MOMENT

There are going to be lonely times in any new situation when you don't know what to expect, or you know all too well what lies ahead. Military wives who experience deployment and reintegration, and wives whose husbands are home due to injury, illness, depression, or lack of direction, may encounter a lonely disconnect from their husbands and the life they knew before having a stay-at-home man.

Sherry, one of the military wives sharing above, wrote a review of Dr. Gary and Barbara Rosberg's book *6 Secrets to a Lasting Love* (faithdeployed.com/2012/03/6-secrets-to-a-lasting-love-a-book -review/). These "six secrets to recapturing your dream marriage" will help all marriages survive a lonely time of feeling disconnected:

- FORGIVING LOVE: heals hurts and helps spouses feel accepted and connected.
- SERVING LOVE: discovers and meets needs and helps spouses feel honored and understood.
- PERSEVERING LOVE: stays strong in tough times and helps spouses feel bonded—best friends for life!
- GUARDING LOVE: protects from threats and helps spouses feel safe and secure.
- CELEBRATING LOVE: rejoices in the marriage relationship and helps spouses feel cherished and captivated.
- RENEWING LOVE: refreshes and supports the marriage bond and helps spouses feel confident and rooted.

GOD'S **LOVE LETTER** TO YOU

*Dear*_____,
   You can be sure of this: I am with you always, even to the end of the age
(Matthew 28:20 NLT; paraphrased).
                                          Your Constant Companion, God

LET'S **PRAY**

God, we need Your presence. We feel empty and alone and don't like
our thoughts right now. Give us pure hearts and minds. Protect us from
the evils of jealousy—thinking others have an easier life. Please bring us
a friend who understands and will stand by us. Amen.

Dealing with Depression

Learning from prior warrior's experiences can spare future warriors
from PTSD and related depression. Educate yourself, family, and
friends about PTSD before, during, and after deployments.
                    — LT. COL. TONY and PENNY MONETTI, *Called to Serve*

Why are you downcast, O my soul? Why so disturbed within me?
   Put your hope in God, for I will yet praise Him, my Savior and
my God.   — PSALM 43:5

JANET'S **JOURNAL**

Dear God,
   You created Dave mellow—he doesn't experience extreme highs or
lows. So I didn't readily notice the signs of depression when we went
through his first layoff. But after months of hearing he was overqualified,
which he interpreted as too old and past his career prime at 50, his
shoulders began slumping and he seldom stood up to his full 6' 4"
height. He stopped shaving, getting haircuts, and taking daily showers.
He wore the same shorts and tank top for days and became content with
sitting on the couch—sometimes staring into space.
   I knew we had a problem and encouraged Dave to exercise and work
out at the gym . . . join a men's Bible study group at church . . . retrain

for a new occupation. Interestingly, after 18 months of unemployment, his next job opportunity surfaced at the gym.

He moved through the second layoff much faster, and since I had breast cancer I don't think he allowed himself time for depression — about work anyway.

He's happily retired now, but still displays some depression symptoms: sleeping late, not caring about appearance, grumpy, short-fused, and a lack of motivation. Maybe he's just taking advantage of having no agenda, but I hope it doesn't last long.

Hanging in, Janet

A STAY-AT-HOME MAN SHARES: *Joseph*

Agent Orange terrified me in the 1970s and 1980s when I saw buddies die — young veterans like me — ravaged by vicious cancers and other disorders. Having Agent Orange posed difficult questions. How could I look my children in the face and tell them I had this dreaded condition? *My children* certainly didn't deserve this. I had waited so long to become a father — many buddies were already grandfathers.

I read on the Internet that Agent Orange can manifest in cancer, diabetes, or neurological disabilities. Mine was neurological. I was to expect a steady deterioration of my nerves, the "end game" unknown. At night as I struggled to sleep, my legs cramped with "shocks" from the bottom of my feet to my calves. My best hope was to stabilize my condition, now mainly located in my legs.

Five years after "the call," I developed Parkinson's. It became frightening to have dinner with friends for fear a tremor would send a glass flying.

A future I had taken for granted was now in doubt. My wife would have none of it. She left our three kids and me.

MENTORING MOMENT

There are hard times and difficult days going through any life transition or change. Even couples who have planned for this day, or want the husband to be home, still have moments when one or the other is feeling down. Those emotionally low times can be very hard on marriages.

In *Honey, I'm Home for Good!*, Mary Ann Cook reports: "According to the National Foundation for Depressive Illness, a third of retirees experience occasional depression. One in six becomes depressed enough to require treatment." Depression isn't limited to retirement or to the husband. A wife could experience depression when suddenly she finds herself a caregiver, alone after a deployment, pinching pennies, returning to work, or just isn't coping well with the new stay-at-home man lifestyle. For an extended list of symptoms, go to page 181 in "Sanity Tools."

If either of you is crumbling under the weight and pressure—especially when displaying signs of desperation or life isn't worth living—seek professional help *right away*. Telling your husband or yourself to "cheer up" or "buck up" won't alleviate depression. Prayerfully find a Christian biblical counselor or speak with a pastor. Locate a church with depression or caregiver support groups. If you're in the military, utilize the services each branch provides.

Don't ignore your feelings. You need each other now more than ever. Pray together and start a journal remembering how God has seen you through previous dark times. This new set of circumstances didn't catch God off guard, and He's not going to let you fall. Hang on tight to Him and to each other.

GOD'S **LOVE LETTER** TO YOU

Dear _____ ,

"*And now, my daughter, don't be afraid*" (Ruth 3:11).

"*Don't be afraid, for I am with you. Do not be dismayed, for I am your God. I will strengthen you. I will help you. I will uphold you with my victorious right hand*" (Isaiah 41:10 NLT).

Your 24/7 Strength, God

LET'S **PRAY**

Abba, Father, we know we're no help to our husbands when we're nagging and wrought with fear, especially when he may be doing the best he can or had no control over the situation. Please calm our fears and change our attitudes. Don't let us sink into the dark hole of depression. Keep us attuned to any negative signs in our husbands. Remind us that we're whole in You. You're holding us together and You'll catch us when we fall. Amen.

YOUR LETTER TO GOD

This transition journey encounters some "bad days," but with God's love and strength, you'll make it through. List what's bothering you and prioritize in order of importance. Talk to God about high priority items and ask Him to show you ways to minimize their negative impact. It's OK to cry out and to cry.

Dear God,   *Date:*

_____

_____

_____

_____

_____

_____

_____

_____

_____

_____

FOR DISCUSSION

1. What waiting room are you in now and how are you handling the wait?

2. Share tips for calming anxious thoughts and sleeping peacefully.

3. Review the signs of depression on page 181. If you're experiencing any indicative signs, what will you do to get help?

Chapter 8:
ENJOYING THE GOOD DAYS

The trash has become a laughing matter. Trash has never been "the man's job" in our house—I've always taken it out. For some reason, my retired husband is now compelled to empty the container and then leave the trash bag in the kitchen instead of taking it outside. I'm reclaiming the job for myself! — NANCY

Hallelujah!
Thank GOD! Pray to him by name! Tell everyone you meet what he has done! Sing him songs, belt out hymns, translate his wonders into music! Honor his holy name with Hallelujahs, you who seek GOD. Live a happy life! Keep your eyes open for GOD, watch for his works; be alert for signs of his presence.
— PSALM 105:1–4 (*The Message*)

If He's OK, I'm OK

My heart beat a little faster when my husband used the word *decorate* in a sentence. It was OK when he decorated the garage, but what would he think of to decorate next? — JOANNE

May your fountain be blessed, and may you rejoice in the wife of your youth. — PROVERBS 5:18

JANET'S JOURNAL

Dear God,
I'll admit it was alarming when Dave started figuring out ways for us to live without him going back to work after . . . if . . . he recovered from his reconstructive foot surgery. He wanted to retire, he was done; but I wasn't ready. Then I thought about the doctor calling Dave *stoic* for continuing in a job requiring so much walking with such a messed

up foot. He never complained. Just put on his work boots and uniform, popped a couple Aleve, and headed out in his pest control truck every day . . . until he could barely walk.

When Dave presented me with a spreadsheet showing we could make it financially if we moved out of California and I took early Social Security, the relief and joy on his face melted my heart—and my resolve that he needed to find another job.

Wrinkles and age lines seemed to shed from his face and I knew there was no going back to before the surgery. Life was going to change significantly. I can't say I threw him a retirement party, but I did start getting on board with selling our home and considering a relocation to another state—Idaho! Yikes, Lord . . . how is this native California girl ever going to make such a drastic move?

Trying to smile, Janet

A WIFE **SHARES:** *Joanne*

I had a long to-do list for hosting our family Thanksgiving. Grandpa, my husband, said he too was preparing for the holiday gathering and also had a very long list. Now I was worried.

"Fix up the garage, dear?" I asked. "Do you mean clear out junk and hoses off the floor so we can eat in there?"

"No," he replied. "I mean—decorate. I've always wanted a good-looking garage like I see in magazines, and now with the family coming, I have an excuse for making our garage picture perfect."

Surely this would bring new meaning to the word decorate.

He began "decorating" by methodically sharpening garden tools and giving their handles a coat of lacquer. Our son suggested Grandpa had too much time on his hands and should get a hobby or be on the golf course.

Next, he cleaned cupboards and drawers, tossed out junk, took old paint and oil for recycling, and removed the eyesore workbench quickly thrown together over 35 years ago. I was surprisingly sad to see it go.

The garage got messier each day. But after hearing his ideas, I could imagine it *eventually* looking great, almost like a magazine. I was beginning to like his decorating idea.

After adding wallboards and patching nail holes, everything received paint, even the cupboards—inside and out. It wasn't the color *I* suggested, but the color our son wanted—light blue, the color of our old car. "Yes, we like blue in the house," I said, "but do you *really* want it in the garage?"

Often summoned to hold on to the rickety ladder, which I grasped tightly fearing both ladder and Grandpa could collapse at any moment, I thought, *I'll buy him a new ladder for Christmas—a very short, very strong one.*

Silver pulls on the cupboard doors looked pretty against the blue paint, and plastic bins stored miscellaneous tools and plumbing supplies. Fresh paint on our ugly old freezer made it look brand new with old sports trophies and a small television adorning the top. An overhead light fixture with a fan replaced the old one, vinyl tile squares adorned the floor, and he assembled and installed a new workbench.

How great the garage looks, actually too nice for cars or projects messing up the brand-new workbench.

His buddies dropped by to see how the project was progressing, but warned me not to let their wives see or hear about it. They feared they would have to "decorate" their garages too.

Grandpa discovered where I stored old pictures. "They'll be perfect for the garage," he insisted. So onto the freshly painted walls he hung my prints, oil paintings, and photographs—along with his old Harley Davidson sign.

As a former aerospace engineer, the final touch to his masterpiece was a photo taken from space. The garage was finally decorated—Grandpa-style. Surveying all he had done, he couldn't have been happier or more pleased with the results. I concurred.

MENTORING MOMENT

As Joanne in the above story learned, sometimes you just have to let your man do what makes him happy, even if you're skeptical. I liked the way she let Grandpa continue developing his decorating ideas, though they differed from hers.

We're not the only ones going through a major transition when our husbands come home. He's accustomed to going to work every day, and then suddenly, his world topples upside down too. Like us, he needs to express his creativity and ideas, and as long as he's not hurting himself or anyone else, it's usually best to let him have his fun and his way.

GOD'S **LOVE LETTER** TO YOU

Dear _____,

Each of you should use whatever gift you have received to serve others, as faithful stewards of My grace in its various forms (1 Peter 4:10; paraphrased).

Graciously, God

LET'S **PRAY**

Lord, help us not to think only about our own space needs, but remind us to give our husbands their space too and allow them to do things they enjoy—even when it conflicts with what we want or we think things should be done differently. Give us patience, compassion, understanding, encouraging words, and above all, love for our husbands. Amen.

We're Having Fun Now!

It took a couple of years to adapt and be happy.　— MICHELLE

The good news is it gets better, but it took four years. Now when he's gone for a long time during the day, I miss him.　— PRISCILLA

On a good day, enjoy yourself.　—ECCLESIASTES 7:14 (*The Message*)

JANET'S **JOURNAL**

Dear God,

We were specific in our requirements for a house in Idaho: not a fixer-upper, since neither of us have those gifts; not too close to neighbors—but not isolated; and maintained roads with easy access in the winter. I needed a quiet writing office set apart from the rest of the house with an inspirational view, but Dave also needed space. Oh, and we wanted to have our young grandkids visit often so we needed a playroom and a safe yard.

Amazingly, You led us to realtors who helped us locate the perfect cabinlike home, only four years old, at a price we could afford in the rural mountains of Idaho. The house has three levels: We can turn the top floor into my office suite, Dave and the grandkids can have their space in the basement apartment complete with kitchenette—quickly labeled Dave's Cave—and the middle level will be our living quarters.

Only by Your grace did we coordinate closing escrow on the California and Idaho homes, downsize our belongings, pack up both cars and a moving van, and make the long road trip to begin our new life.

Let the fun begin . . . we're moving to Idaho! I hope we know what we're doing.

Nervously, Janet

A WIFE **SHARES**: *Sheila F.*

I see a very relaxed, stress-free, retired Mike. It took him about two months to adjust to the idea of being free of the corporate routine. It was surreal when they carted off his company car and we realized this was the end of 38 years in medical sales!

We went to lunch to celebrate. It was so hard to believe the time had come after all the years of working! Mike said he didn't realize the stress he had lived with until he didn't have it anymore!

We really are enjoying getting up at our leisure, having our coffee, watching the birds, and enjoying the mountain vistas. It's so nice to have relaxing mornings. We're walking together, going to lunch, taking day trips, and enjoying friends.

Also, having a hobby in common is good for us. We both play golf so we can be out in nature, staying active.

We've had many out-of-town friends and family visit, and with Mike retired, we can thoroughly enjoy the time without the stress of a job.

MENTORING MOMENT

There can be many celebratory moments—over-the-top and rip-roaring—but some celebrations require a choice, especially if your husband being home is not by choice. God does change mourning to dancing again when we change our perspective: despair to delight, deflation to elation, unhappy to happy, discouraged to encouraged, disappointment to enjoyment. Celebrating doesn't minimize loss, but it does emphasize the Cross.

In Philippians 4:4, Apostle Paul, who had endured many unpleasant hardships, wrote from prison, "*Rejoice in the Lord always. I will say it again: Rejoice!*" Regardless of your circumstances, God is still on His throne watching over you. That alone is reason for exuberant joy and casting aside whining doubts.

Sacrifice often accompanies major transitions and our attitude plays a major role in how we *choose* to adapt. Dave and I had no idea everything God had planned for us once we let go of the old life we had known for so many years and decided to embrace the new unknown life God laid out before us.

Whatever brought your husband home—an illness that maybe only promises you a short time left together, a job loss that resulted in the loss of everything, a husband traumatized by a brutal tour of duty, a planned or unplanned retirement, a home office—you both need to find or create moments of joy. Happiness hinges on our circumstances, but inner joy does not.

GOD'S LOVE LETTER TO YOU

Dear _____,

"*There is a time for everything, and a season for every activity under heaven: . . . a time to weep and a time to laugh, a time to mourn and a time to dance*" (Ecclesiastes 3:1, 4).

Joyfully, God

LET'S PRAY

Oh, Jesus, don't let us ever miss an opportunity to celebrate the good things You bring into our lives. Remind us to celebrate anniversaries, birthdays, holidays, graduations . . . regardless of the trial we're enduring at the time. And help us never minimize the wonderful things You do for us *every* day and the painful sacrifice You made just for us. Remind us to celebrate Your birth and resurrection and to work at keeping fun and light-heartedness in our marriage. In Jesus' name, Amen.

There Are Humorous Moments

Alan had to wear heavy elastic stockings for blood circulation. He said he'd never wear shorts again, but that was short-lived with our Texas summers. There have been a few good jokes about his "thigh-highs," but he never complains about washing his own hose.　　— NANCY

We cannot really love anybody with whom we never laugh.

— AGNES REPPLIER

A cheerful heart is good medicine, but a crushed spirit dries up the bones.　　　　　　　　　　　　　　　　— PROVERBS 17:22

JANET'S JOURNAL

Dear God,

Prior to Dave's retirement, we seldom shopped together. Occasionally we'd pick up a few items but never a major shop — certainly not for my personal items like underwear and bras. Living in rural Idaho, the closest town for shopping is an hour away, so our lists are long and we go together in one car . . . to the same stores. I never noticed before how many couples are shopping together in the middle of the day on a weekday! Most of them look our age or older, and I give a knowing nod to a wife trying to explain to her hubby why they need baking chocolate instead of a chocolate candy bar.

As we enter a store, Dave starts the interrogation: "What do we need here and how long will it take?" He's a hunter/gatherer; I'm a browser/explorer. I like to leisurely *experience* stores, but he navigates the shopping cart quickly through the aisles on a mission.

Occasionally, I break free by sending him to look at the garden or electronics department or to put gas in the car, and I quickly duck into a dressing room. Soon my cell phone is playing "his ring tone"—the theme song from *Top Gun*— "Where are you?" "Trying on bras," I whisper.

If I take too long, he calls again to tell me he's waiting outside on a bench or in the car: "Take your time." Which I interpret as: "I can only sit out here in the heat/cold so long."

In the grocery store, I've tried giving him his own cart and sending him off on a hunting expedition for simple items like tortillas. He returns with "wraps," explaining: "This store doesn't have tortillas." I chuckle. Then I came up with something more challenging: Find a barbecue sauce without high-fructose corn syrup. That bought me about a half hour, and he was so proud when he returned victoriously with the *one* acceptable brand, after reading every label on the shelf! Then he was ready for his next assignment.

Chuckling, Janet

A WIFE **SHARES:** *Janet*

The following cute "retired husband" story isn't true, even though it might resemble a "Mr. Harris" or husband you know (I edited a bit):

After my husband retired, I wanted him to accompany me on trips to Walmart. Unfortunately, like most men, he found shopping boring and preferred to get in and get out. Like most women, I love to browse. Yesterday, I received the following letter from the local Walmart:

Dear Mrs. Harris,

Over the past six months, your husband has caused quite a commotion in our store. We cannot tolerate this behavior and must ban you both from the store. Listed below are our complaints, documented by video surveillance cameras, against your husband, Mr. Harris:

1. June 15: He took 24 boxes of diaper wipes and randomly put them in other people's carts when they weren't looking.
2. July 2: Set all the alarm clocks in Housewares to go off at five-minute intervals.
3. August 4: Went to the service desk and tried to put a bag of M&Ms on layaway.
4. August 23: When a clerk asked if they could help him, he began crying and screamed, "Why can't you people just leave me alone?" EMTs were called.
5. September 4: Looked into the security camera and used it as a mirror while flossing his teeth.

6. October 3: Darted suspiciously around the store loudly humming the "Mission Impossible" theme.
7. October 21: When an announcement came over the loud speaker, he assumed a fetal position and screamed, "Oh no! it's those voices again!"

And last, but not least:

8. October 23: Went into a fitting room, shut the door, waited a while, and then yelled very loudly, "Hey! There's no toilet paper in here." One clerk passed out.

MENTORING MOMENT

While writing this chapter, the following cute joke circulated on the Internet and Facebook:

FRANCHISE OFFER:

Husband Day Care Center
Need time to relax?
Need time to yourself?
Want to go shopping?

Leave your husband with us!
We look after him for you!
You only pay for his drinks.

Of course, "drinks" would be nonalcoholic. I'm sure you're chuckling and thinking, *What a great idea! Why didn't I think of that!* Sometimes, you just have to laugh. Maybe at yourselves—maybe at the situation. You're not laughing off your problems, making light of them, or laughing at your husband, you're just giving both of you permission to have a good day.

We recently attended the retirement party of a former retired lieutenant colonel who had been an army aviator—helicopter pilot. When his kids were growing up, he had made laminated to-do lists for their chores. So as a spoof on Dad, his wife and the kids put together a laminated "retirement" to-do list for him. He took it good naturedly, and everyone at the party enjoyed passing around the list and adding ideas to it. For a good laugh, check out the list on page 185 in "Sanity Tools" and maybe get some ideas for making your own to-do list.

Did you know your body relaxes when you smile? Plant a big smile on your face and try being tense or stressed. You can't do it. Many studies substantiate that laughing is healthy: It's good for healing and it's contagious. Sometimes I laugh so hard trying to tell Dave something, he can't help but join in even though he doesn't have a clue why we're laughing.

Les and Leslie Parrott suggest in *The Love List* that you should study your spouses' funny bone. They write:

> Let's face it, no spouse is immune to stress. We all feel like we're coming unglued at times. Wise experts agree that the best way for anyone to cope is with a good laugh.
>
> One of the reasons many couples never reach their "laughter potential" is because they have never taken humor seriously. Sounds strange, but to bring more laughter into your relationship, you need to know what makes your husband or wife laugh. After all, each of us has a unique sense of humor.
>
> Maybe your partner likes a sarcastic wit. Maybe it's slapstick that makes him or her laugh. Or maybe it's the old classic sitcoms like *The Andy Griffith Show*. Wherever his or her funny bone is located, find it and use it—at least once a day.

Cherish funny times—there will be some—often overlooked or minimized by the seriousness of a situation. Laughter helps keep everything in perspective. The Bible assures you will laugh again: *"The nights of crying your eyes out give way to days of laughter"* (Psalm 30:5 *The Message*). Life is never *all* bad or *all* good: don't let the serious eclipse the humorous.

GOD'S **LOVE LETTER** TO YOU

Dear _____,

"Rejoice! Celebrate all the good things that God, your God, has given you and your family" (Deuteronomy 26:10 *The Message*).

The Author of Laughter, God

LET'S PRAY

Lord, we've been serious for so long and we're not smiling much lately. Help us indulge in the kind of laughter we experienced before setting out on this journey. Please put joy back into our hearts as we focus on good times and not just on disappointments or the difficulty of this transition. Lighten our burdened shoulders and spirit. Give us eyes to see and a willingness to acknowledge funny moments in our day. Remind us to cherish the many blessings You've already given us. Amen.

YOUR LETTER TO GOD

Record good experiences so when the hard days come, and they will, you can look back and remember what God and others have done for you.

Dear God,   *Date:*

_____

_____

_____

_____

_____

_____

_____

_____

_____

_____

_____

_____

_____

_____

_____

_____

_____

_____

_____

FOR **DISCUSSION**

1. What have you had to let go of to allow your husband to have his space?

2. How are you keeping fun and perspective in your relationship?

3. Describe humorous moments in hubby being home.

Chapter 9

KNOWING WHO IS IN CONTROL

Spinning Out of Control

The Lord has shown me so many things about myself. I never thought I was selfish, but take away my quiet alone time and my emotional string begins to unwind; now both our "strings" are frayed and unraveling.

— BETH

Those who do not control themselves are like a city whose walls are broken down.   —PROVERBS 25:28 (NCV)

JANET'S JOURNAL

Dear God,

At first, everything was fun settling into our mountain home and rural environment. Dave loved his Man Cave in the basement apartment and I set up my office on the top floor.

We chose this house specifically to provide me quiet writing solitude and a space for Dave to call his. But just as I feared, even with the middle floor between us . . . things started unraveling quickly . . . and I began to feel out of control of my work environment, which quickly spiraled into me questioning, "What have we done?"

I had two books due soon after we arrived. My publisher graciously gave me an extension for the move, but as soon as we were unpacked, I needed to get back to work writing. We purchased pager phones to communicate between Dave's Cave and my office and we each had a cell phone—which was the first problem. Engrossed in a thought, suddenly the shrill phone pager or the theme song from *Top Gun*—my cell phone ring tone for Dave—pierced the silence. He wanted to tell me what he saw on the Internet . . . that the deer were eating his birdseed . . . he was going to get the mail or take the trash to the dump.

Then, Lord, You made me with an uncontrollable startle reflex. It doesn't take much of an unexpected noise to cause a heart-pounding, fight-or-flight, screaming response. We had a workable system in California—as Dave walked into the house, he would announce, "I'm home!" Since he wasn't coming home from work anymore, I guess he thought my startle reflex went on retirement too. Quietly, he enters my office, and when I turn to investigate the shuffling sound, I jump out of my seat screaming while he stands sheepishly smiling at me—not fazed by my near heart attack.

I worry I'll never get my writing groove back. Is this going to work? I don't want Dave to feel like a prisoner in his own home. How are we going to combine my need for quiet to write with his right to be in his own home? Is it possible?

Out of control, Janet

A WIFE SHARES: *Veola*

"We're refinancing the house," my husband told me over the phone while I was in the middle of my stress-filled workday. This news was the last thing I expected. But since he'd been home, many things had changed.

My former policeman husband had been home a year now (due to his work-related injury) "helping" take care of household duties while I went to work. We've struggled to figure out our new situation. House cleaning became an immediate issue: Within two weeks, he hired someone. My first reaction: "You never hired a maid for me, why do you get one?" Once I got over those feelings, it was a grateful relief and I look forward to coming home from work to a sparkling house on Tuesday afternoons.

Food was another out-of-control issue: The children were accustomed to my cooking. Born and raised in Barcelona, Spain, my husband's idea of a meal included as much seafood as possible—something I rarely cooked despite knowing he liked it. Once he started doing the meal preparation, mussels, octopus, and all types of fish became a customary part of our dinner menu. The children reacted with tears and more tears.

Tears became a common part of our home for several months. It wasn't just the kids. I shed my fair share also. Work stress after being out of the field for almost ten years, missing my children after being home with them for eight years, and adjusting to a husband going through an identity crisis kept us all on our knees. Only an utter dependence on God got us through those first months.

MENTORING MOMENT

Almost every story I received from a wife with a stay-at-home man, no matter what the cause of his being home, had some element of spinning out of control. Both spouses experience an emotional rollercoaster: highs . . . . lows . . . hopefulness . . . disappointment . . . anticipation . . . anxiety . . . fear that maybe this isn't going to work. Children still at home experience and internalize their parents' emotions.

Fear ignites out-of-control feelings, triggering a survival instinct to regain control, culminating in a tug-of-war over who is in control. Max Lucado confirms in *Fearless*, "Fear, at its center, is a perceived loss of control. When life spins wildly, we grab for a component of life we can manage: our diet, the tidiness of a house, the armrest of a plane, or, in many cases, people. The more insecure we feel, the meaner we become. We growl and bare our fangs." Does this describe you lately?

On your own, you can't control fear, but God can. Even if you're angry with God, be real with Him because He already knows how you're feeling—He's God. Ask for His help. You can't stay on a roller coaster for long without losing your balance, equilibrium, and maybe your lunch; and you can't stay in an emotional out-of-control state for long either. Soon everything and everyone will upset you and the onslaught of emotions could destroy all you hold dear.

Going through a crisis of emotion without God is like being on a rollercoaster that never stops until it crashes. If you don't have God at the center of your life, go to page 174 and pray the prayer that will stop your world from spinning out of control. If God is in your life, give Him back the controls. Do you feel your feet getting back on the ground? Steady now, you might still be a bit shaky.

GOD'S LOVE LETTER TO YOU

Dear _____,

"*Do not be afraid, for I am with you and will bless you*" (Genesis 26:24 NLT). "*Be still, and know that I am God*" (Psalm 46:10).

Always in Control, God

LET'S **PRAY**

Lord, we detest feeling as if we're losing our sanity. We ask the Holy Spirit living within us to help us regain stability in our emotions and actions. As dark as things seem, we want to believe it won't be like this forever. We trust Your plan for our life. We know the stress and upheaval we're experiencing isn't getting us any further toward our goal of living peacefully together with our husbands. We're breathing in the Holy Spirit and exhaling out the friction and pain consuming us. Thank You for the peace only You can provide. Amen.

Controlling the Controllable

It was tough learning to share my kitchen—my husband *loves* to cook, probably because he *loves* to eat! I'm grateful for the food channel which has taught us to work together cooperatively in meal preparation. We've come a long way and now actually enjoy cooking together.

— DEBBIE

If I keep my eyes on GOD, I won't trip over my own feet.
— PSALM 25:15 (*The Message*)

JANET'S **JOURNAL**

Dear God,

Dave and I prayed together asking for Your wise counsel before discussing a workable solution for 24/7 life in our new home—which also houses my writing office and About His Work Ministries. We agreed to "house courtesies" we could both honor on writing days:

1. Unless an emergency, don't call or page while I'm writing. Email is fine so I can read and respond during a break or save to discuss over dinner. Check.
2. Announce when you're coming up the stairs into my office.

For the most part this has worked well. However, just as I was writing this section, Dave "forgot" about my startle reflex and scared me out of my office chair. We're making progress.

3. Last one out of bed makes the bed. Check.
4. We fix our own breakfast and lunch. I make dinner and Dave cleans up. Check.
5. I wash and dry, he sorts and folds laundry. Check.

Lord, help us remain flexible, understanding, and focused on serving each other.

Feeling more in control, Janet

A WIFE SHARES: *Debbie*

I see God's merciful hand on our "both-at-home" journey. He allowed us to make the transition gradually. I was actually the one who intruded into my husband, Jerry's, work-from-home world. He was gaining momentum in his real estate business, and I was looking for a way to leave my full-time job and care for our new grandson. Jerry suggested my assisting him would achieve both our needs and desires. And so it began.

Jerry loves attending sales meetings and socializing with co-workers at the real estate office, so I mostly had my space. When working at his home office, he enjoyed even more companionship with me working with him!

It was tough learning to work our business together. I'm the support part of the team— making sure all the i's are dotted and the t's crossed—I need my space and alone time. In the beginning, I quit, and he fired me five times a day. We're very different and had to learn how to play to one another's strengths.

After seven years, we gave up our real estate office space to work exclusively from home. 24/7 of joyful bliss—Not! We do everything together: three meals, business, home improvement projects, premarital counseling ministry, and for recreation we go on motorcycle rides together—me on the back—no control!

Jerry's involvement in the community and two men's Bible studies has helped us adjust. He's out a lot and I get my at-home alone time. I too am involved in a Bible study and work out at the gym regularly. Fortunately, we each have created some space.

MENTORING MOMENT

Coexisting at home together requires surrendering control. Sit down together and *each* list friction areas. You'll probably see some issues are petty and others are significant. Prioritize your lists in order of importance and work at mutually agreeable solutions. For example, Alice said her husband turns the television volume too high, a common complaint of wives with stay-at-home husbands. Instead of complaining or trying to get him to turn it down, Alice bought "TV ears" for her husband, which allows him to mute the TV. Nancy also agrees these are a blessing in her husband's ears if she's concentrating on something, but she warns earphones do silence conversation: "We've had to sort this out during our walks together."

Dave has a TV and DVD and CD players in Dave's Cave, so he can watch his sports games and play his John Denver anniversary album all he wants; but if he's upstairs watching TV in the evening and I'm still working, he mutes the TV and uses subtitles. It works.

A common dispute involves control of the kitchen and cooking—an area many women claim as their domain, not readily shared with anyone, especially their husbands. Anita says she resents her retired husband's desire to start cooking: "This is *my* kitchen. It's been my kitchen all these years. He won't let me run the dishwasher until it's completely full and even rearranges the dishes! It's like me going into *his* office and sitting in *his* chair."

I would actually love Dave to cook—especially when I'm on a writing deadline—but he prefers doing dishes, so I'll take it.

Unwillingness to relinquish "my" tasks and routines resembles children unwilling to share a toy—"Mine!" That's how childish we look to the Lord. Let your husband help in areas where he's expressed an interest. Allow him to show initiative, providing gentle guidelines where pertinent. For example, "Please don't put my lingerie in the washer with your Levi's." I laughed at the tweet by speaker and author Shelia Walsh where her husband Barry "helped" with the laundry and put her cashmere sweaters in the dryer. She tweeted asking if anyone knew of a Chihuahua needing sweaters.

Sometimes you just have to smile and offer grace.

GOD'S **LOVE LETTER** TO YOU

Dear_____,

"*My grace is sufficient for you, for my power is made perfect in weakness*" (2 Corinthians 12:9).

Your Stronghold, God

LET'S **PRAY**

Lord, it isn't easy relinquishing areas we've felt were our responsibility. Help us not be control freaks! Give us compassion for our husbands as they seek new areas of competence to excel in and feel worthy and valuable. Guide us in how to be encouragers and not squelchers of their initiative, while still enjoying our own areas of expertise. It's an intricate balancing act, and we don't want to tip the scales. Keep us ever in tune with You and our husbands. Amen.

Temptations and Distractions

My husband played Wii golf for hours on end. Thankfully, he's working now and is (almost) retired from the Wii! — CHERI

Keep watch and pray, so that you will not give in to temptation. For the spirit is willing, but the body is weak!

—MATTHEW 26:41 (NLT)

JANET'S **JOURNAL**

Dear God,

Dave has discovered the world of Internet shopping. When he was working, he seldom got on the computer and did little shopping—virtually or personally. Then when he was housebound with his foot surgery, he spent hours on the computer and a new world opened up to him when he discovered Amazon and Google Web search. He mainly did research and comparative pricing until he retired and we moved to the mountains of Idaho where the nearest shopping is an hour away.

Packages of various sizes and shapes started arriving at our door on a regular basis. I put a halt to him signing up for Amazon Prime, where for an annual fee he could receive two-day *free* shipping on all Amazon orders. I knew this would lure him into even more shopping "because the shipping is free"—even though the item isn't!

My solution to this Internet shopping enticement has been to keep him busy with projects for the ministry. In the spring and summer, he'll be outside planting and caring for a garden and the yard—and maybe a part-time job at the local golf course will lure him away from the computer—although golf could become another temptation and distraction.

Reeling him in, Janet

A WIFE **SHARES:** *Debbie*

I have to confess my biggest complaint about Jerry working from home and our 24/7 togetherness is his addiction to email! He spends a lot of time at his computer for our business, so I give him the benefit of the doubt that he's actually working and not just looking at email.

I'm the housecleaner around our home (my choice, I'm picky). Jerry usually pitches in by vacuuming, at the very least. But when he gets into his email addiction, he doesn't even notice I'm cleaning or might need help. I try to address the issue with him before I become angry and resentful, but sometimes it sneaks up on me, and before I know it, an argument ensues.

When I bring to his attention that he's spending too much time on email and I could sure use some help, he's quick to apologize and reprioritize. This is still my biggest issue with us both being at home, but it's getting better all the time.

MENTORING MOMENT

We'll talk in chapter 11 about the importance of a stay-at-home man redefining a new purpose for this time of life—determining what God created him to be and do. If the two of you hadn't anticipated and planned for this season, your husband can find himself with nothing to do but surf the Web, watch TV, play with smartphones, or numerous electronic devices and gadgets—there's a virtual world available to him and some of it isn't good or healthy. Men, including Christian men, can be tempted and lured into the sordid virtual world of pornography—especially if they're home alone.

Keep communication open with your husband. Help him find a hobby or an opportunity to volunteer in the community or at your church. Sitting down all day, either on the couch or in front of the computer, isn't healthy mentally or physically. If he's able, encourage him to join a gym or take walks together.

The important thing is not to ignore a problem and hope it will go away. Your husband's addiction or temptation can sneak up on him and you. Address your concerns with him, without being confrontational, and offer solutions. If your husband isn't receptive, ask your pastor to talk with him.

GOD'S **LOVE LETTER** TO YOU

Dear _____ ,

No test or temptation that comes your way is beyond the course of what others have had to face. All you need to remember is that I, God, will never let you down; I'll never let you be pushed past your limit; I'll always be there to help you come through it (1 Corinthians 10:13 *The Message*; paraphrased).
Righteously, God

LET'S **PRAY**

Lord, please watch over our husbands and protect them from addictions and temptations. Guide them in how to occupy their time and energy in ways that please You. Give us kind and understanding words to help direct our husbands in the paths of righteousness for Your name's sake. Amen.

Surrendering Control

I have to let go of trying to control what I can't change. I can only control my attitude—I can't change my husband. — ALICE

I could not survive this season of unemployment if I didn't know God was in control. — BETH

Let the morning bring me word of your unfailing love, for I have put my trust in you. Show me the way I should go, for to you I lift up my soul. — PSALM 143:8

JANET'S JOURNAL

Dear God,

"Retirement" sounded old and finished to me. . . . I wasn't ready to go there, so I resisted this for Dave too. I don't ever intend to retire—I hope to write and speak until You, Lord, take me home. What would Dave do to stay productive during retirement? I remember his dear parents living sedentary lives watching TV and reading while sitting in their matching rocker-recliners Dave bought for them. I feared that was Dave's vision for his retirement when he bought his own rocker-recliner!

In the past, when I heard women talk about their husband's "medical disability," I felt sorry for them: *Poor thing, he probably sits on the couch while you do all the work.* Now *I* have a medically disabled, retired husband—somehow I always thought he would take care of me.

I moved into this season of our life reluctantly and apprehensively. Like most of the world, we had watched our retirement funds dwindle during the recession. We had planned to be in a good financial position when we retired, but we weren't there now. Could we live on my writing and speaking income and Social Security?

These thoughts kept me up at night until I turned everything over to You, remembering You're our Provider, not Dave. You have seen us through layoffs, career changes, downsizing, illnesses, a major move. . . . You would see us through retirement. You have it all under control.

Retire-less, Janet

A WIFE SHARES: *Sally*

Early in our marriage, my husband's desire to control matched with my independent bent to control was a recipe for disaster. Deployed regularly while in the military, Walt was away more than home, which left me unfettered in running things *my* way.

During those first years, as days approached for Walt's returns, a sense of dread accompanied my excitement to have him home. The first few days were generally tense and loud with the ensuing battle of wills as he proceeded to upset all my daily routines and schedules, especially concerning the care of our horses.

Reminding myself of 1 Corinthians 11:3, *"The head of every man is Christ, the head of every woman is man, and the head of Christ is God,"*

I begrudgingly stepped back, but in anger. My "submissiveness" became self-destructive, reflecting in our relationship. Counseling with our pastor provided insight into how Walt ticked, but we still had a strained marriage.

Then Walt had a longer deployment and something happened—answered prayers. Absence makes the heart grow fonder, but it also provides an opportunity to be ourselves. Walt had to let go of the reins and allow me to do the "manly" jobs at home. I didn't have the usual inner struggle about him being upset if I took care of something he considered "his job."

When he called home (Internet and cell phones not an option then), I had a list of questions. He offered guidance, which I could follow, or take my own course of action.

Over the following months, God worked in each of us separately. I had to step up and attend to things. Although it was hard accomplishing everything and working full-time, it felt good to be the old me again. Perhaps Walt realized that my caring for the home wasn't a threat because on his return, he looked at me differently—almost like he saw the independent, stubborn woman he fell in love with. And I realized how much I needed him, how much easier life was when we pooled our strong wills into a team.

It still needs tweaking, but Walt's returns are much more joyful; the dread is gone. I make sure things in the house are in order, and he asks me about my daily regimen, particularly with the horses. He always changes the regimen within a few days, but at least he asks and attempts to do it my way.

Prayer and communication are key. Spontaneity is fun, but we find coordinating our agendas regularly makes life much more enjoyable and allows us to work side-by-side and laugh at each other's stubbornness. Things we do:

- Establish a home calendar we both check each day.
- List "honey do's" to see what each other wants to accomplish and how to help, be it staying out of the way or remaining flexible.
- Chat early about the day's activities to accommodate each other's needs.
- Allow for each other's quiet times—mine is morning until after my second latte, Walt's is evenings on the deck.

- Find ways to make the other laugh—surprise each other.
- Thank each other for the things we do.

MENTORING MOMENT

Kay Warren has a mantra I quote in my book, *Dear God, They Say It's Cancer*: "I want to control the controllable and leave the uncontrollable to God." As much as we sincerely try to embrace this practice, we often take back things as fast as we give them to God and to each other.

Life with a stay-at-home man will *always* require relinquishing control in some area. Even if you work outside the home, home is your domain, and you ran it while he ran his world. Now the two worlds have collided and need merging. Military couples experience this on a regular basis. During deployment, the wife takes over the controls at home; but when her husband returns, she may need to relinquish areas where she's become quite competent. Maybe he'll be happy to let her continue doing some things, or maybe he'll feel more at home taking back familiar areas he was in charge of before he left. For suggestions on renegotiating leadership after deployment, see page 178 in "Sanity Tools."

The key to living cohesively in all situations is to remain flexible and humble. The husband still is the head of the household, whether he's home or not. While the wife is to submit to her husband, the husband is to cherish his wife, and both remember the ultimate Head of the home is God. If both spouses are acting in a godly, Christlike way, they'll see that God's been the one in control all along!

All the wives in this book saw God at work when they let Him do His work. Every story, including ours, is a story of surrendering control to God.

GOD'S LOVE LETTER TO YOU

Dear _____,

"Out of respect for Christ, be courteously reverent to one another.

"Wives, understand and support your husbands in ways that show your support for Christ. The husband provides leadership to his wife the way Christ does to his church, not by domineering but by cherishing. So just as the church submits to Christ as he exercises such leadership, wives should likewise submit to their husbands.

"Husbands, go all out in your love for your wives, exactly as Christ did for the church—a love marked by giving, not getting. Christ's love makes the church whole. His words evoke her beauty. Everything he does and says is designed to bring the best out of her, dressing her in dazzling white silk, radiant with holiness. And that is how husbands ought to love their wives. They're really doing themselves a favor—since they're already 'one' in marriage" (Ephesians 5:21–28 *The Message*).

The Head of Your Home, God

LET'S **PRAY**

Abba Father, You have our attention. We surrender to You and to Your will for our stay-at-home man. We're broken in all the right places and we're ready to do things Your way. Amen.

YOUR LETTER TO GOD

Have you surrendered control of your life to God? If so, write about it so you can return and read what you wrote whenever you're tempted to take back the reigns. If you haven't completely surrendered control, then tell God what's stopping you. List out-of-control areas and cross off everything you can't do anything to change. Feel the reigns slipping out of your hands.

Dear God,   *Date:*

_____

_____

_____

_____

_____

_____

_____

_____

_____

_____

_____

_____

FOR **DISCUSSION**

1. Where are you "spinning out of control"?

2. What are you attempting to control that should be surrendered to God's control?

3. Where do either of you need help in overcoming temptations or distractions? Ask for prayer.

Chapter 10:
GRIEVING THE LOSSES

A dear friend's husband received a leukemia diagnosis a month into his retirement and passed away within the year. Her jobs are now many and she makes decisions by herself—the renovation of the cottage they intended to share, the multiple issues of a slab leak—and the joys of the pending birth of triplets to her son and twins to her daughter. Her husband would have loved it!　　　　— NANCY

My days are filled with grief.
I am exhausted and completely crushed.
My groans come from an anguished heart.
You know what I long for, LORD;
*　　you hear my every sigh.*

— PSALM 38:6, 8–9 (NLT)

The Grieving Process

A man's work is his identity. He's invested through his time and effort, and he experiences a traumatic loss when it's stripped away or comes to an end.　　　　— JEAN

Job stood up and tore his robe in grief. Then he shaved his head and fell to the ground before God.　　　　—JOB 1:20 (NLT)

JANET'S JOURNAL

Dear God,

Dave's layoffs were scary, and I think he grieved over them more than I did. He felt the loss and rejection, but I always knew he would find something else. When Dave had his foot surgery and there was talk of possibly losing his job again, I knew he didn't want to reinvent himself and find a new career at his age. He was ready officially to retire with no regrets.

I wasn't ready for him to retire. We had planned for him to work until he was 67, and he was only 64. When his foot took over a year to heal and his company did let him go, I had to accept that he wasn't going back to work again . . . ever!

I grieve the plans we had for those next three years. I grieve the end of his working season of life and I grieve plummeting into a season I'm not ready for yet. I grieve the sense of security his job provided. I grieve who we were as a productive, contributing-to-society couple.

God, I need to get my perspective back and see his retirement through Your and Dave's eyes and not just mine. I know You're not done with us yet. . . . I'm just processing what life's going to look like now.

Grieving, Janet

A WIFE SHARES: *Jean*

My husband, a hardworking engineer by education and experience, worked for a major oil company for over 33 years. He didn't want to retire, but was caught in a traumatic downsizing. Within two months, he began two new careers.

His main panic concerned finances. It's a huge adjustment going from a bimonthly autodeposit payment into your checking to living on your savings. A financial planner informed us that the large sum of money we had accumulated wouldn't last to the end of our "planning horizon," unless we radically changed our lifestyle.

I'm sure this is what prompted my husband's stress, sleeplessness, and ultimately, the two new jobs he now offices out of the house. So he's here—*always* here. We live in a two-story house and the upstairs is now his "office," except for my sewing room.

He wasn't the only one traumatized. I've always been involved in volunteer work, and at the point of his "retirement," I was greatly involved in a volunteer situation taking more than its fair share of time. But I was clinging to it for dear life because giving it up would bring about so much "togetherness." Don't get me wrong, we have a strong marriage and I wasn't unhappy—just didn't want to become too overwhelmed at home, if you know what I mean. We were both swimming in the deep end of the pool in uncharted waters.

A few months prior to my husband's forced retirement, I was diagnosed with cancer. Both our lives were turned upside down in a very short period of time.

MENTORING MOMENT

Regardless of what brought your husband home, there's a sense of loss of the known—the life you had both become accustomed to—even if you did not have the best of circumstances, you knew what to expect. Look at the steps of grief in "Sanity Tools" on page 181 and locate where you are now. Grieving is a process—keep moving through the steps.

You also may be grieving your image of God and your expectations of Him. Perhaps you're angry with God or your husband. Anything buried alive has energy, which eventually erupts explosively, just like unresolved feelings—toward God, your spouse, or others. Beleaguered Job in the Bible understood this concept when he said, *"Even if I say, 'I'll put all this behind me, I'll look on the bright side and force a smile,' all these troubles would still be like grit in my gut'"* (Job 9:27–28 *The Message*).

The losses you're mourning will take time to work through, so allow time to grieve completely, and then make a conscious decision to move on in the direction God leads you as a couple. Chris Tiegreen writes in *The One Year Walk with God Devotional*, "In the midst of our pain, God speaks promises. In the far reaches of our grief, He reaches even farther. He promises comfort to those who know the grief of this world. He offers Himself in comfort."

GOD'S LOVE LETTER TO YOU

Dear _____,

"Blessed are those who mourn, for they will be comforted" (Matthew 5:4).

Your Comforter, God

LET'S PRAY

Oh Jesus, this is such a difficult journey, and we could never make it without Your love and support. Forgive us our doubts and anything we have done out of anger or sadness. When will the grieving and feeling of loss end? When will we wake up and be happy to see a new day? Hold us, Lord. We need our mourning turned to dancing again, soon. Amen.

Feeling Guilty

I feel guilty comparing my husband with other retirees and all the things they do with their time and talents. — ALICE

How is it I had an easier time with him gone on deployment for a year than I'm having with him home every night? — LAURA

Then I let it all out; I said, "I'll make a clean breast of my failures to God." Suddenly the pressure was gone — my guilt dissolved, my sin disappeared. — PSALM 32:5 *(The Message)*

JANET'S JOURNAL

Dear God,

Dave took to retirement like he'd been waiting for it his entire life. I knew he had worked hard to support us all those years and he probably did deserve some downtime. I felt guilty for wanting him to keep working. I hounded him to find something part-time as soon as he could walk. I thought it would help us financially, give him purpose, and give me space and time to write while he was at work — even if just for a few hours a day. I was so used to having uninterrupted time to myself that his constant presence almost felt smothering.

I know it's his home and he has a right to be here too — just not full-time. Right after our move to Idaho, I was panicking as the days slipped by toward my deadline and writing was going slowly. Dave was also frustrated not knowing how he fit into our new life, so one Friday he announced he was going to town for the day!

I felt guilty at the relief I experienced as he drove out of the driveway — like he used to do every day — and I reveled in the luxury of a whole day to myself at home, since "town" is now an hour away. Many widows, wives with deployed husbands, and single women would love to have their husbands underfoot — what's wrong with me? I love my husband. Am I just a bad wife and person?

Guiltily, Janet

A WIFE **SHARES:** *Sheila L.*

My husband transitioned about a year ago from full-time in the office to full-time telecommuter. It's wonderful—and sometimes, it's frustrating.

When Rich drove to work each day, he left at 5:30 A.M., giving me two hours of uninterrupted solitude before I had to leave for work. I could write, manage household tasks, pay bills, think, and read. With his office relocated to upstairs, he's *always* here, and I am interruptible.

For example, he'd come downstairs for more coffee and engage me in conversation when I was trying to write. I'd lose my train of thought and be frustrated, then feel guilty at my frustration. I have young widow friends who would give anything for their husbands to interrupt them one more time.

I love my husband. I want to be interruptible for him, but I also need some breathing space. I hesitated to mention my frustration because I didn't want him to feel rejected. When I finally spoke up, he got it.

We've recently relocated my computer/writing space to a quiet corner of our bedroom. If I close the door, he doesn't interrupt me. It's bliss.

MENTORING MOMENT

Each time I read a story or interviewed a wife with a stay-at-home man, I felt some of my guilt dissipating. Other wives needed space and me time too. I wasn't a bad wife and neither are you. Michelle expressed all our feelings when she told her husband, "I love you, but you have to find something to do with yourself. I love you, but leave me alone!"

Interestingly, Michelle's husband, Bob, felt guilty when he was out having a good time with his buddies while she was home "working," which often was gardening she loved doing on her own! Michelle wanted him to enjoy himself while she enjoyed her alone time, but he wanted to come home and "help" her. Perception and clarification are essential elements of relieving guilt and opening up the channels of communication.

If you're a military wife, you might feel guilty struggling with your husband being home. You've been longing and praying for this day and he's home safe—maybe not the same man who left—but you want to be grateful. Why then is it so hard? Allow time for both of you to adapt to his homecoming and bathe your relationship in love, patience, and prayer.

Most wives with a stay-at-home man said it took a couple of years—sometimes four or five or longer—to adapt and be happy. Some of you are thinking, *I don't think I can stand it for a couple of months, not to mention years.* Or, *We need to work things out before he deploys again!*

Take a deep breath, pray hard, and keep reading. There's hope and you *will* make it. Sometimes we need to be the ones to adjust and other times we need to help our husbands find purpose and a new routine or way of coping with his new normal.

Conviction, not *guilt*, is from God. Confess your feelings and concerns to God and to your husband and talk about mutually agreeable ways to resolve the issues.

GOD'S **LOVE LETTER** TO YOU

Dear_____,

"You'll be able to face the world unashamed and keep a firm grip on life, guiltless and fearless. You'll forget your troubles; they'll be like old, faded photographs. Your world will be washed in sunshine, every shadow dispersed by dayspring. Full of hope, you'll relax, confident again; you'll look around, sit back, and take it easy" (Job 11:15–19 *The Message*).

Your Guilt-Buster, God

LET'S **PRAY**

Lord, we know feeling guilty isn't productive or beneficial. Help us resolve the source of guilt and replace those feelings with joy and love for our husbands. Give us ideas and tools for helping them have meaningful lives in this new phase of life and flood us with compassion, understanding, and courage to make the changes we need to make in ourselves. Amen.

Husbands and Wives Process Loss Differently

I'm grateful we serve in a premarital counseling ministry, which keeps us reviewing and studying God's design for marriage. My biggest takeaway from the program is learning to appreciate each other's differences. Instead of saying, "Lord, why can't he be more like me?" I understand God made us different so we can complete one another.

— DEBBIE

God works in different ways, but it is the same God who does the work in all of us. — 1 CORINTHIANS 12:6 (NLT)

JANET'S JOURNAL

Dear God,

Lord, You made Dave and me with opposite personalities and reactions to most situations, especially times of loss. When Dave gets uptight, he gets quiet, reclusive, and doesn't want to talk about the issue while he's processing—maybe for days. That makes me think he somehow rationalizes everything will just go away if we don't discuss it. I want to talk things out until we arrive at a satisfactory solution—quickly, so we can move on.

I'm afraid at our house the saying rings true: When Wiffy's happy, everybody's happy; and when she's unhappy—well, nobody's going to be happy until she's happy again.

Wiffy, Janet

A WIFE SHARES: *Vanessa*

Ideally, I would like to say, "Dear God, thank You, he's working!" Then my husband wouldn't be on a kidney transplant list. And ideally, I would be a wife whose bicycle accident hadn't resulted in over 111 broken bones, damaged heart valves, amputations of 10 toes, and 27 surgeries.

As Greg grieved the loss of his dream to play college football and I grieved the lost plan of becoming a cosmetologist and bearing and raising children, we learned to depend on God. We've dealt with these lost dreams by involving ourselves in ministries not requiring serious time commitments, yet allowing us to use the different spiritual gifts God's given each of us.

I'm an encourager, so with my physical issues freelance writing from home works best for me. Greg has the gift of giving and is less physically limited, so he volunteers and hands out Gospel tracks at church and local food ministries. Mostly, he enjoys making people laugh.

Greg's gift of giving is another reason I'm glad he's home. Often, Greg is sweet to remind me, "I want to help you." I don't object. Although we have a different definition of "clean," I let him do the things I'm not so picky about and he likes most doing. After sending Greg to the market with a list and my cell phone nearby, he comes home telling me about the interesting people he met and new friends he made. It's like another day of "Greg's Adventures."

God created Greg an extrovert and me reserved, so Ecclesiastes 4:9–10 works well for us.

MENTORING MOMENT

Personality differences and the way God created you will determine how you each grieve the loss of the life you knew before your man came home, and you may each be grieving something different.

A man commonly goes into his figurative cave, tuning out emotionally as he tunes into television, computer games, the office, work, reading, surfing, golf, sports—whatever helps him avoid talking or thinking about the problem. Women need to talk. A husband in his figurative cave leaves his wife feeling rejected, alone.

Most men don't stay in their caves forever—they need to process issues in their own time and space and then they reengage. Wives can give them their much-needed space by finding another listening ear with a family member, best friend, or mentor.

Differences of opinion also may arise in how to achieve this next phase of life. Dave and I find it's best not to make major decisions until we're both in agreement and have peace—then we know we're making the decision God wants for us. God put the two of you together for a specific reason. Be patient, pray for each of you to experience peace and unity. God made you unique as man and woman, but you fit perfectly together in the union of marriage.

GOD'S LOVE LETTER TO YOU

Dear_____,

"Two people are better off than one, for they can help each other succeed. If one person falls, the other can reach out and help. But someone who falls alone is in real trouble. Likewise, two people lying close together can keep each other warm. But how can one be warm alone? A person standing alone can be attacked and defeated, but two can stand back-to-back and

conquer. Three are even better, for a triple-braided cord is not easily broken"
(Ecclesiastes 4:9–12 NLT).

Your Third Cord, God

LET'S PRAY

Lord, we're trying to be wives who learn to celebrate differences with our husbands and not judge them for reacting differently. Help us remember husbands and wives deal in their own way with transitions in life and marriage. Grow us closer to our husbands and don't let anything pull us apart. Guide us with Your wisdom and give us courage to face the future united in body, soul, and spirit. Amen.

YOUR LETTER TO GOD

Are you grappling with a future different from your plans and dreams? How are you coping with the unexpected changes? How is your marriage doing? Do you feel any clarity or are you still in a state of confusion? Use this time to pour out your heart to God. Let Him give you a vision and a hope for your future.

Dear God,   *Date:*

_____

_____

_____

_____

_____

_____

_____

_____

_____

_____

_____

_____

_____

_____

_____

FOR **DISCUSSION**

1. Go to the steps of grief on page 181 and determine which step applies to you now. What can you do to move to the next step?

2. What's making you feel guilty and how can you confront and alleviate those feelings?

3. How do you and your husband process problems and how do you view each other's differences?

Chapter 11

DISCOVERING A NEW FOCUS AND PURPOSE

Amazingly, we were able to focus on the positive aspects of having Richard at home. He enjoyed spending more time on his hobby—music composition—and I enjoyed his help with the school carpool and laundry. We found a new rhythm as a family. — CHAR

I'm not saying that I have this all together, that I have it made. But I am well on my way, reaching out for Christ, who has so wondrously reached out for me. Friends, don't get me wrong: By no means do I count myself an expert in all of this, but I've got my eye on the goal, where God is beckoning us onward—to Jesus. I'm off and running, and I'm not turning back. So let's keep focused on that goal, those of us who want everything God has for us. If any of you have something else in mind, something less than total commitment, God will clear your blurred vision—you'll see it yet! Now that we're on the right track, let's stay on it. Stick with me, friends. Keep track of those you see running this same course, headed for this same goal.
— PHILIPPIANS 3:12–17 (*The Message*)

Changing Focus

My husband struggled to maintain focus—the less he had to do, the less he did. It was painful. — CHERI

Learn to be content and focus on "the positives." — ALICE

Here's what I want you to do: Find a quiet, secluded place so you won't be tempted to role-play before God. Just be there as simply and honestly as you can manage. The focus will shift from you to God, and you will begin to sense his grace. —MATTHEW 6:6 (*The Message*)

JANET'S JOURNAL

Dear God,

When Dave was working, he focused on his job. When he was home due to a layoff, he focused on finding a new job. We set up a desk in the girls' old room and he worked at finding work. When he was home with foot surgery, he sat at that same desk focused on getting back on his feet and *possibly* back to work.

When thrown abruptly into retirement, he focused on financially surviving—selling our house, buying a new one, and orchestrating the zillions of details surrounding the move. When we arrived in our new home and new state, he focused on getting us settled and established in an environment the antithesis of what we had always known.

Once we settle in . . . what will be the next focus . . . for the rest of his life? We really haven't discussed that and I don't think Dave feels the need to "focus" anymore. His mantra is, "Let's just take it day-by-day and see how it goes."

Focused, Janet

A WIFE SHARES: *Priscilla*

When my husband first retired, we were busy with church activities and a trip to Florida. We didn't have any free time and both wondered: *When's the retirement going to hit?*

Once we stopped traveling, it hit me: He didn't have a lot to do. He watched movies. It quickly became apparent he no longer had a routine. After being a stay-at-home wife and mother for 28 years, *I* had a routine I wanted to keep.

I realize he had to make changes too. He was used to being with people all day. I got used to living by myself during the day. I need my quiet time. He needs to be with men, just chatting. I'm glad he found a group of men to meet with on Monday mornings, but he wanted me to go with him; I didn't want to. It's hard because he wants me to do things with him. It's an adjustment for us both.

He said, "I can help you with the housework so we'll have time for fun." He does vacuum, and when I ask for help with the dishes, he always does them. But you need to tell men what to do because they don't readily see things on their own.

It's better in the summer because he has the yard and golf, but that's what he talks about *all* the time. When he monopolizes the supper conversation, I don't say anything. Just let him talk.

I've learned how selfish I am. Giving up my routine was a sacrifice I wanted to make for the man I married. I do love him and he loves me. When I'm more flexible, I'm always glad and it works out. I still need to go more with the punches—he says I don't do that very well. I don't think either of us does because we're old and set in our ways.

I'll go with him to the coffee shop sometimes because it's nice to be together, and we do have a different conversation at Cabin Coffee than at home in the living room.

MENTORING MOMENT

Most women say one of the hardest things is watching their previously busy husbands suddenly "unbusy." Or those men with home offices who now lack the structure and discipline provided by going to an office. Television, computer games, newspaper, Wii, Facebook, surfing the Web or the waves—whatever distracts or entertains them—can be big deterrents to setting goals or having productive days.

Alice said retirement was different than she expected. She thought for sure her husband would find things to do—maybe develop a new hobby or go fishing more, which he loves. She feels a void, but when she questioned her husband about his lack of interests and the hours he spends just staring into space on the porch, he cautioned her: "Don't worry about it. I'm not worried."

Wives, even those retired, usually still stay busy with home responsibilities—housekeeping, laundry, grocery shopping, family, meal planning and preparation, social activities, yard work . . . and maybe a hobby or two. However, Alice admitted that watching her husband so relaxed was a reminder she needed to change her focus and let go of some things—slow down too. They talked about him needing to pitch in and help around the house so she could have free time to enjoy with him.

Your husband may want you to shift your focus as he has done. A fair response would be, "If you want me to change focus from maintaining the home to more leisure time, I need your help." Remember, though, as Priscilla pointed out, don't expect them to know where you need help—my husband confirms you must tell men specifically what and how you want something done. Don't set both of you up for failure by letting him "figure it out on his own."

GOD'S **LOVE LETTER** TO YOU

Dear_____,

If you are humble I will lead you in what is right and teach you my ways. If you keep My covenant and obey my decrees I, the Lord, will lead you with unfailing love and faithfulness (Psalm 25:9–10 NLT; paraphrased).
Your Refocus, God

LET'S **PRAY**

Lord, it isn't easy changing our focus. Father, give us willing minds and hearts to see the doors You're opening to take us in a different direction from where we've spent the majority of our lives. Help us keep our focus on You and our husbands, not on our circumstances and ourselves. Amen.

Uncovering God's Purpose

Mike is now semiretired, working part-time for a golf company and leading the Sports N Action program he started at church. I think it's critical for him to have something he really looks forward to doing, as well as serving in ministry.   — SHEILA F.

We look at this Son and see God's original purpose in everything created. For everything, absolutely everything, above and below, visible and invisible, rank after rank after rank of angels—everything got started in him and finds its purpose in him.   —COLOSSIANS 1:16 (*The Message*)

JANET'S **JOURNAL**

Dear God,

I've always thought life without purpose is meaningless. Purpose gets you out of bed in the morning and sets the course for your day. I've been asking Dave what he thinks his purpose is now that he's retired, but I don't think he knows. He's sleeping late and pretty much doesn't start his day until noon and then wonders why the days go by so quickly.

I asked him what his idea of retirement was and he said it happened so fast . . . remember Lord he's a processor . . . he really didn't have a chance to think beyond "playing a lot of golf . . . at least three times a week."

Unless he's *working* at the golf course, Lord, *playing* just doesn't seem very purposeful.

Purposely, Janet

A WIFE SHARES: *Deola*

My husband's identity crisis was one of our biggest struggles when he had to take early disability retirement and I went back to work. He had no idea what he would do with himself. At first, he watched television all day. Then, he transferred his energies to his smartphone, spending hours downloading applications and playing games. Online chess became a standard.

I realized something my training in psychology had already taught me—a man needs something to do. It's all about purpose. Now that he's home, he has to redefine his life purpose.

I began giving him household to-do lists. He took on the grocery shopping, errands, and homework with the kids. But it wasn't enough. It wasn't "manly." He didn't mind doing these things, but they clearly didn't give him purpose. He needed more. And he still does.

After being at home for over a year, he's still restless. So we're refinancing our home. It gives him something to do. He's also changed our cable company. We have a new telephone carrier. We're changing our life insurance. I'm thankful he has a relationship with the Lord Jesus who will, in many ways, define his identity for him.

MENTORING MOMENT

In *Retired with Husband*, Mary Louise Floyd addresses the many baby boomers who are retiring en masse in the upcoming years. She calls the wives who grew up in the baby boomer era "superwomen" who need to help their husbands find purpose in the unprecedented long life they have before them in their "second adulthood." Floyd describes the initial loss of purpose many men feel when coming home:

Anyway, when your husband realizes he's lost his space, called "the office," from which he exercised power and control and derived his identity, he feels bereft. Even if your husband's job involved traveling, or if his "office" was cyberspace, it was still his space, his sphere of influence. He held sway over this space, which he filled with his life's purpose for ten thousand days (call it ninety thousand hours!). In his psyche, a void has replaced this lost domain. No longer can he attach nine hours a day to the space that defined his purpose.

Floyd's comments apply even if your husband isn't a boomer or retired. Before coming home full time, he found his identity in the answer to the proverbial question: "What do you do?" His answer now: "retired," "disabled," "out of work," "working from home," or "home from deployment." When asked, "Where is your office?" Typical answers: "the garage," "a bedroom," "a closet," "the basement," "What office?"

People often ask my husband, "What did you *used* to do?" His answer clarifies who he *was*, but entreats the unspoken question: Who are you *now*? Another demeaning question: "What do you do with yourself all day? Aren't you bored?"

A man often equates his purpose to what he did/does for a living, where he did/does it from, and how many hours he spent/spends at it, but there is so much more to purpose than our work. Floyd asks the question: "So how does she [the wife] move him from being controlled by a schedule that defined his daily purpose toward an unscheduled life in which *he* defines his purpose?"

The answer to Floyd's question: A wife encourages her husband to let *God* define his purpose. When I tell people I want Dave to have a purpose-filled retirement, they often look at me quizzically. Our former pastor Rick Warren explains what I'm talking about in *The Purpose-Driven Life:*

The purpose of your life is far greater than your own personal fulfillment, your peace of mind, or even your happiness. It's far greater than your family, your career, or even your wildest dreams and ambitions. If you want to know why you were placed on this planet, you must begin with God. You were born *by* his purpose and *for* his purpose.

So the *first* thing a wife can do is pray for her husband to seek God's purpose for this season of his life. Encourage him to pray about his "calling." What does God want him to do with his life now?

Then give him space to seek and find God's purpose and calling:

- Allow *him* to select an "office" space he can call his. He might want it in the garage, a workshop, guest room, basement, attic, or maybe build on a house addition or "man cave." Let him "decorate" or not—it's his domain. We fondly call our basement apartment Dave's Cave.
- If his space doubles as a guest room: How many times do you have guests? Compare to his every day need for it. Put in a futon or sofa couch for the grandkids or guests and let him take over the room.
- Give him a calendar and once a month review upcoming activities and appointments for both of you and keep him updated on changes or additions so he feels a part of the home activities.
- Ask which of the household duties he wants to help with, and when a new project or purchase arises, put him in charge of doing the research and planning.
- Ask him to develop a budget for your new "lifestyle."
- Let him run errands. It gives him a chance to get out of the house.
- Unless you love doing the yard work, ask if he would like to take over the upkeep of the yard and outside maintenance or plant a produce garden.

Pray with and for your husband to find his purpose and his space.

GOD'S **LOVE LETTER** TO YOU

*Dear*_____,

    "My purpose is to give life in all its fullness" (John 10:10 NLT).

                           Jesus Christ, Your Lord and Savior

LET'S **PRAY**

Lord, please help our husbands find purpose in their current situations. Remind them to find their identity in Christ alone and not let the world define their purpose or significance. You created each of us for a purpose and You have a plan for our lives. Give us wisdom and discernment in helping our husbands discover a new God-given direction and purpose for their life and give each husband a willing, receptive heart. Amen.

We're in This Together for Better or Worse — But Not for Lunch

It's very simple. It's give and take and compromise.

— WILBUR FAISS on his 80th wedding anniversary

He's my soulmate. I love him now more than I ever did, which says a lot. Those married awhile understand this means going through the good, the bad, and the ugly. — BETH

They are joined fast to one another; they cling together and cannot be parted. —JOB 41:17

JANET'S JOURNAL

Dear God,

Dave and I have experienced many major transitions, but nothing prepared us for 24/7 life together. I thought it was "understood" that while Dave navigated through retirement, I'd keep on doing what I always did—writing and speaking. Instead, Dave acts like we're on an extended vacation or an unending weekend. We do live in the mountains now, and when we used to go to our mountain cabin in Idyllwild, California, I usually prepared three meals a day and had more leisure time. But Lord, this is our *home* now, not a weekend getaway!

Those first few days, when Dave so sweetly asked if I was ready for lunch or what was I planning for lunch or did I want him to make me lunch, I was thinking: *Lunch? I don't do lunch! I'll eat a leftover or grab a bite at my desk . . . or not. . . . I can't stop the creative juices to eat lunch.*

Still, from my office I could hear Dave come up the stairs from Dave's Cave, make his lunch in the main floor kitchen, and the screen door slam behind him on his way out to the front deck to eat. Distracted from my writing, I unconsciously and uncontrollably waited for the sound of the screen door upon his return back to the kitchen to clean up his dishes and retreat downstairs. This process took around two hours!

Finally, we had the discussion that something needed to change. Dave's Cave is fully equipped with a kitchenette including refrigerator, stove, microwave, sink—the works. We agreed he would prepare his lunch down in *his* kitchen and take the outside route to the deck or eat downstairs. When I'm not writing, or can take a break, I'll join him. Whew, lunch really caught me off guard.

Can't do lunch, Janet

A WIFE SHARES: *Jean*

One incident about my husband losing his job and setting up shop in our home is now very funny, but wasn't at the time. To keep things organized and coordinated—my husband still sets an alarm and carries out the same routine as when he went to the office to work. You can set your watch to his schedule.

By 8:00 A.M., he's in "the office," which is now upstairs in our home, ready to begin his day. On the first day of his new life, he bounded down the stairs about 11:30 and said with an enthusiastic smile, "What's for lunch?" I was in the kitchen, but lunch wasn't my agenda. My mind quickly went into fast-forward and I could see the rest of my life fixing one meal after another—cooking, cooking, and cooking. . . . I didn't respond in a positive way. Should have said, "Wherever you're taking me," or possibly, "This kitchen is closed for lunch."

What I said was, "Lunch! I do lunch with my friends!" Ouch. He looked crushed and I instantly knew I had mishandled this new phase of life.

I'm happy to say we've worked things out and even occasionally have lunch together. We're into a smooth, flexible rhythm and in a very good place. Slower—not always a bad speed. I learned to guard my relationship and to be sensitive.

MENTORING MOMENT

Before you're thinking, *Poor Dave has to stay down in Dave's Cave*, it's actually a fully furnished apartment described by overnight guests as a "luxurious suite." Our kids were worried when we first nicknamed it Dave's Cave until they saw how lovely and spacious it is with a big TV, his desk and computer, and comfy furniture. Dave *really* is very happy with his own space.

I could have included many more stories about stay-at-home husbands expecting lunch and their wives' shocked reactions. Peanut butter and jelly worked for the kids when they were home and we wives usually finish leftovers on the run . . . graze . . . or maybe go out to lunch with a friend. Now he's home and wanting lunch, every day!

Alice's husband sits down at the table waiting for his lunch. Priscilla said that her husband retiring from *his* work, added to *her* work—like making lunch. Anita's husband agreed to make his own breakfast and lunch, but he wanted dinner ready at 5:00 P.M., too early for her. Michelle's husband puts in his "order" for what he wants for meals. Other wives complain about cleaning and straightening the house more because he's home all day dirtying and messing it up, or having more laundry since he isn't using the cleaners anymore.

And on the stories went . . .

Instead of feeling resentful or overwhelmed, put into perspective issues like lunch or helping with household duties and discuss with your husband in the same way you would a major decision or planning a trip—talk it out.

Most husbands were used to eating lunch somewhere—maybe driving up to a takeout window, or sitting in a restaurant and ordering, or going to the lunchroom and eating the lunch you packed. They don't know how to change that pattern unless you help redirect them to making their own lunches now or going out with the guys. One husband, who went from working in an office to working out of the home, still gets in his car and drives to lunch. It was what he always did and it feels right. I'm sure it feels right to his wife too!

GOD'S LOVE LETTER TO YOU

Dear _____,

   I, God, made marriage. My Spirit inhabits even the smallest details of your marriage. And what do I want from your marriage? Children of God, that's what. So guard the spirit of marriage within you (Malachi 2:15 *The Message*; paraphrased).

Presiding Over Every Area of Your
Marriage, God

LET'S PRAY

Lord, there are so many transitions and new areas to address. We love our husbands. Help us understand what they're going through and not make it all about us. Give us a willing, pliable attitude and direct us in how to approach our husbands without breaking their spirit. Amen.

You, and He, Need an Outlet

When Bob retired, he bought two snowmobiles. I didn't like those smelly things, but I didn't want him to go alone. I was so happy when he met other snowmobilers and I didn't have to go anymore! Then he started making friends who play golf and I gained some space.

— MICHELLE

Oh, how sweet the light of day,
And how wonderful to live in the sunshine!
Even if you live a long time, don't take a single day for granted.
Take delight in each light-filled hour.

— ECCLESIASTES 11:7–8 (*The Message*)

JANET'S JOURNAL

Dear God,

Walking has always been my physical and emotional outlet. I love walking and talking with my girlfriends or with You, God. I try to walk every morning, rain or shine. Walking just gets the endorphins flowing and life seems good!

After his foot surgery, Dave couldn't take walks and he wasn't even sure he could play golf, his retirement dream. He needed something to do—an outlet.

When our six-year-old granddaughter started taking guitar lessons, she inspired Grampa to clean off 15 years of dust from his two guitars and start strumming again down in Dave's Cave. Now, he's taking online lessons!

He's also involved at church making phone calls for the monthly men's breakfast, attending morning and weeknight Bible studies, and watching football games with a group of friends. He's even managed to fit in a couple of golf games and bought a new club to help him play better. So maybe playing golf is in his future.

When we moved into our new home there was snow on the ground, but when it melted in the spring, plants started popping up so Dave asked our neighbor Anita, a seasoned gardener, to point out plants versus weeds in our almost-one-acre yard! In California, we paid a gardener—Dave never lifted a shovel or pushed a lawn mower. I had no idea, and I don't think Dave did either, gardening and yard maintenance would become his new hobby.

To everyone's surprise, Dave planted and cultivated a produce and herb garden. I'm amazed watching him tend to tomatoes, herbs, berries, trees, flowers . . . he actually has a green thumb! When he brings in his "crops," I praise him and put them to good use.

My stay-at-home man has become Farmer Dave!

The farmer's wife, Janet

A WIFE SHARES: *Anita*

When Gary took an early retirement and was *inside* the house all the time, I started gardening *outside*. I enjoyed it so much, our entire yard became a lush garden and I began selling plants. At first, Gary just sat in the house while customers roamed through our yard.

As word of my "plant business" spread throughout our community and beyond, I needed help. Several of my friends assisted, but one day when they weren't available, I asked Gary to help take money, and he actually enjoyed it. I got him a money belt, and soon he had learned my "spiel" and could help sell. It took a while, but he finally got in the groove and caught on. Sharing a hobby we both liked drew us closer together.

MENTORING MOMENT

A stay-at-home man can become a wife's full-time job, as he tries to make her his new hobby! When does she retire from the household management or being a caregiver or parenting? Here are several creative ideas to help both of you adjust to, and even enjoy, this stay-at-home man season:

- Develop individual hobbies, and if possible, do one together.
- Both learn something you've always wanted to know how to do.
- Leave the house on your own at least once a week.
- Plan a weekly or monthly date together. Put it on your calendars.
- If still parenting, join a babysitting co-op, trade off babysitting with friends, or if finances permit, hire a sitter and go have fun.
- If you're caring for a sick or disabled husband, ask a friend or family member to stay with him and do something for you—not just running errands and chores.
- Exercise daily.
- Serve as a volunteer for a charitable organization or a ministry.
- When a husband retires, the wife retires from one home chore. Her choice.

GOD'S **LOVE LETTER** TO YOU

Dear_____,

Each of you should use whatever gift you have received from Me to serve others, as faithful stewards of God's grace in its various forms. If anyone speaks, they should do so as one who speaks the very words of God. If anyone serves, they should do so with the strength God provides, so that in all things God may be praised through my son, Jesus Christ. To Me be the glory and the power forever and ever (1 Peter 4:10–11; paraphrased).

Creator of Recreation and Service,
God

LET'S **PRAY**

Father, awaken in our husbands, and us, a desire to do something new or start a project that could become a ministry. Give us a desire to serve others. Thank You for the gift of ideas and creativity. Please free us from guilt or concern about seeing this as wasting time. Amen.

YOUR **LETTER** TO GOD

Talk to God about any feelings you've had regarding your work increasing or the adjustments you've made to accommodate the new "togetherness."

Dear God,   *Date:*

_____

_____

_____

_____

_____

_____

_____

_____

_____

_____

_____

_____

_____

FOR **DISCUSSION**

1. What new purpose or "outlet" have you explored and how has your focus changed?

2. How have you resolved the "lunch" issue or something similar requiring extra work?

3. Describe how you're honoring your "better or worse" marriage vows.

Chapter 12

RELYING ON GOD

As we persevere through our deployment and reintegration, we'll continue embracing the real pain of how hard it is and continually strive to rely on God for strength. — SHERRY

So we're not giving up. How could we! Even though on the outside it often looks like things are falling apart on us, on the inside, where God is making new life, not a day goes by without his unfolding grace. These hard times are small potatoes compared to the coming good times, the lavish celebration prepared for us. There's far more here than meets the eye. The things we see now are here today, gone tomorrow. But the things we can't see now will last forever.
— 2 CORINTHIANS 4:16–18 (*The Message*)

Our Faith Has Been Tested

It would be easy to slip into "Why me?" I will not. I will take my medicine and pray that this aging stay-at-home father enjoys as many sunsets as God grants me. As I fight this fight, I know my fate is fully in God's hands. — JOSEPH

Now faith is being sure of what we hope for and certain of what we do not see. — HEBREWS 11:1

JANET'S JOURNAL

Dear God,

Learning to live together in retirement wasn't the first time You've tested Dave and me. Blending a family had its challenges and Dave's job losses weren't fun. Making drastic lifestyle changes helped us realize how little we can live on, but how much we need You!

My recurrences of breast cancer and Dave's disability brought home how temporary and fragile our lives are, but how strong You are when we're weak. We know You would never leave or forsake us.

When we first moved to Idaho, I wasn't sure I would pass this latest test. I love my husband so much and know without a doubt You brought us together, but something seemed different—we weren't in synch with each other or our new life and roles.

It seemed as if You were putting us through the refining fire to take our marriage to a deeper level of trust, understanding, love, and compassion to prepare us for our future journey into an unknown stage of life—together 24/7.

Christians need each other and need to share how we make it through rough spots and life transitions. I wonder if You were bringing me to a place in life so I could finally write *Dear God, He's Home!* I pray we passed this latest test and are ready for You to use us to help other couples transitioning to a stay-at-home man.

Faithfully yours, Janet

A WIFE SHARES: *Karen O'Connor*

My husband announced one day, "I think it's time to retire now that I'm 70." His sudden decision took me by surprise. He loved retail and he was good at it. Men of all ages came from all over the county to purchase shoes from Charles, the shoe guy!

At first, I was happy for him: no more running up and down stairs in the storeroom lugging heavy shoeboxes. No more early and late shifts. But then, I thought about myself. I'm a writer and I need solitude to do my work. I enjoyed my time alone for most of my career. What would it be like to share office space and the telephone? I wondered if he'd expect a hot lunch every day. This new model for our lives definitely tested my faith—in God, my husband, and myself.

MENTORING MOMENT

You may be thinking: *If God loves me, why isn't He making this transition easier or helping us adjust? Why doesn't He change our circumstances—or change my husband?* Then you feel guilty for waning faith in God and in your husband. It's not easy waiting on God's response to your situation.

Faith believes in a God we can't see or hear. Sometimes God tests our faith by making us wait longer than we would like or He goes silent for awhile or puts us in uncomfortable or uncharted territory, but He never stops believing in us—keep believing in Him. God honors faithfulness. Nothing is unexpected to God. Ask Him to reveal your part in His sovereign plan, and He'll do the rest. Military wife Penny Monetti says in *Called to Serve,* "When the external conflicts multiply, and they will, Tony and I have learned to reach out to God, knowing that we can triumph over any challenge when we rely on Him."

When plans seem unclear, wisdom waits. Act on God's *certain* promises, not *chancy* probabilities. Remember: God is the solution, not the problem.

GOD'S **LOVE LETTER** TO YOU

*Dear*_____,

Stay on your toes. Satan has tried his best to separate all of you from me, like chaff from wheat. I've prayed for you in particular that you not give in or give out. When you have come through the time of testing, turn to your companions and give them a fresh start. (Luke 22:31–32 *The Message*; paraphrased).

Faithfully Yours, God

LET'S **PRAY**

Lord, thank You for Your faithfulness and love. We love You Lord and we love our husbands. Remind us we are women of faith, up for any challenge You send our way. You are our stronghold and our strength. Amen.

In God We Trust

"Dear God, please show me You're at work in our situation," I begged, as things seemingly got worse. God immediately began to answer this prayer for Richard's job search.   — CHAR

Lord of Hosts, happy is the person who trusts in You!
—PSALM 84:12 (HCSB)

JANET'S JOURNAL

Dear God,

I'm sure Dave and I wouldn't have made it through the trials and valleys of our life together if we hadn't committed from the beginning that divorce would never be an option and we would put Your Son, Jesus Christ, at the center of our marriage. We learned early on we couldn't be each other's everything or make each other happy all the time.

Even when maintaining confidence in the other's decisions was difficult, we both put our confidence in You, knowing You were trustworthy. I can't imagine how a marriage makes it without You.

Trusting God, Janet

A WIFE SHARES: *Beth*

Being the wife of a middle-aged man out of work is a calling all its own. You don't want to add to your husband's pain, humiliation, or frustration as a man God intended to provide for his household. So much of a man's identity comes from his job. His self-esteem and value resemble strings wound together into a big ball of work defining him. Now, the once tightly wound strings are beginning to fray and unwind.

It's easy trusting in God's provision while you have a regular income. Yet the truth is He is our provider regardless of who signs the check or who puts the food on the table—we clearly understand this now. God has kept us covered and warm and we haven't missed a meal—many people today cannot say the same.

My husband knows the Lord. We've had periods where we spend time together in prayer and devotions, which are doubtlessly better than when we don't spend time inviting the Lord to be our all in all.

God is not a man and does not lie. He is the hope of our future, no matter what the circumstances, so I put my trust in Him and continually ask for His mercy and grace to help in times of need. The needs are great, but He is greater.

MENTORING MOMENT

It's hard trusting God's plan when we want what we want when we want it, and He doesn't seem to be coming through. The true test of faith is when we have no idea what God is doing, but we trust Him anyway—faith under fire.

Trust is a vital component of any relationship, but it's essential in your relationship with the Lord. You cannot profess to love the Lord with all your heart, mind, and soul and not trust Him. So trust Him now with your marriage and life transitions. God sees the bigger picture. While not everything that happens *is* good, God can use everything that happens *for* good. He will—you can count on it.

GOD'S **LOVE LETTER** TO YOU

Dear _____ ,

Do not let your hearts be troubled. Trust in God; trust also in me, Jesus (John 14:1; paraphrased). *Trust God, from the bottom of your heart; don't try to figure out everything on your own. Listen for my voice in everything you do, everywhere you go; I'm the one who will keep you on track* (Proverbs 3:5–6 *The Message*; paraphrased).

I AM Trustworthy, God

LET'S **PRAY**

Father, we are human, but You are holy. We are fallible, but You are invincible. We aren't always trustworthy, but You can *always* be trusted. We want to trust the decisions our husbands are making. Please speak to their hearts and help each one put his whole trust in You and not in a job or his own abilities. Amen.

Praying Expectantly

While on temporary duty, my husband asked via Webcam, "How can I pray for you?" This one question laid the foundation God used to bind us together. We began to share those deep-seated concerns tugging at our heartstrings and brought them before the throne of grace together. We laughed and cried. Prayer forged an intimacy we had never experienced before. — SHERRY

We constantly pray for you, that our God may count you worthy of his calling, and that by his power he may fulfill every good purpose of yours and every act prompted by your faith.

— 2 THESSALONIANS 1:11

JANET'S JOURNAL

Dear God,

I'm so glad Dave and I started the practice of praying for each other's day every morning and praying together again before bed. When Dave was still working, our morning sendoff was to hug and pray. Now that he's home and I get up earlier, I have to make the conscious effort to break away from writing and go down to say good morning and pray. I can only imagine how our prayer time has spared us unknown hardships and brought unity to our marriage, as we put each other's prayer needs before our own.

My heart warms and softens when I hear Dave praying for my health or for You to give me the words to write or speak. Thank You, Lord, for listening to our prayers and helping us hear Your answers—even those we weren't expecting.

Prayerfully, Janet

A WIFE SHARES: *Deborah*

The turning point for us was one Sunday when we *had* to make an important decision and we couldn't come to an agreement. Ken declared a day of prayer and fasting. We sat out in the garden on our deck, read the Bible, and prayed together. During those hours, God broke me to the point where I could finally say, "Not my will, but Yours, Lord."

From that moment on, things started plunking into place: My husband and I found the joy we'd always had in our marriage. Ken's new business from home has provided more income each month, and the rest has always been met somehow (sometimes in ways we believe are miraculous). Most wonderful of all, I have *not* been able to worry. Sometimes, on the rare occasions I wake up in the middle of the night, I'll lay there and actually try to worry. I can't! Peace floods over me as I remember all God has done during this time, and I fall back asleep almost laughing at the absurdity of it!

We thought we lived frugally before Ken lost his job, but we're living on almost half and we're about twice as happy as we've ever been, and that's pretty stinkin' happy! I just *love* God's math! God never failed either of us.

MENTORING MOMENT

Persistent prayer helps resist doubt and restores faith that God can, and will, answer you according to His Word. Cries to God are more to convince ourselves, not Him, that He'll meet our needs—maybe not our "wants". Worship, prayer, and reading God's Word remind us of His unfailing power and love for us. Throughout this book, you've been personalizing and praying Scripture. Praying God's Word back to Him is one way to know you're praying God's will and not just your own will.

Early in our marriage, Dave and I learned the importance and blessing of praying together as a couple "in one accord." When making decisions, we pray until both agree and have peace. The number of Christian couples who admit they don't pray together dismays and alarms us. When asked why they don't pray more with their wives, husbands often say wives can be intimidating or critical. There's no correct way to pray, so wives, lighten up and praise a husband humble enough to pray with you. Read together "Tips for Praying as a Couple" in "Sanity Tools" on page 183. I wrote about the value of praying as a couple in *Praying for Your Prodigal Daughter*:

> Most couples who regularly pray together, including Dave and me, say it's the most intimate experience in their married relationship—even more personal than physical intimacy. Yet some couples are more comfortable naked than speaking to God in front of each other. Don't deny yourself this wonderfully intimate time of prayer together. Once you start, you'll wonder how you ever got along without it.

Hugging is our favorite prayer position, but often we sit next to each other and hold hands. In the morning, we're praying for each other's day, but it's also the time to pray for family or personal issues, and we pray together again at night before going to sleep. This spiritual habit has seen us through tough times and probably warded off untold perilous experiences we never knew we escaped.

Sherry in the opening quote realized the value of praying by Webcam with her deployed husband. If you're apart, be creative with Skype, Facebook messaging, texting, email, or phone when possible. If you can't communicate directly, coordinate time zones to pray for each other at the same time.

If praying as a couple is a new experience, now is a perfect time to start. Your initial prayers probably will be for the current situation. However, as you become more comfortable with this intimate time with God, and each other, you'll be sharing all your praises and pleas. It's the best way to heal a hurting marriage, strengthen a marriage going through a trial, or grow closer together. God doesn't always answer prayer the way we expect, so pray as Jesus did, *"Everything is possible for you. . . . Yet I want your will not mine"* (Mark 14:36 NLT).

Prayers may center on *our* interests, but God answers with *His* interests. Pray your desires, but check your motivation. An answer we don't like is still an answer.

GOD'S **LOVE LETTER** TO YOU

Dear _____,

The Holy Spirit helps you in your weakness. For example, you don't know what I, God, want you to pray for. But the Holy Spirit prays for you with groanings that cannot be expressed in words. And I, the Father, who knows all hearts, knows what the Spirit is saying, for the Spirit pleads for you believers in harmony with My own will (Romans 8:26–27 NLT; paraphrased).

Hearing Your Petitions, God

LET'S **PRAY**

Lord, there are times when we just don't feel like praying for or with our husbands. When those times come, give us the tenacity and courage to pray anyway and to initiate prayer with them. When things look the worst, we need to pray persistently to ward off Satan's attempts to discourage us into thinking prayer won't make any difference. Cast those thoughts out of our minds and fill us with the hope and peace only You can bring. Amen.

Drawing Close to God and Each Other

Today we are more united to Christ individually and together.

—VANESSA

But as for me, how good it is to be near God! I have made the Sovereign LORD my shelter, and I will tell everyone about the wonderful things you do. — PSALM 73:28 (NLT)

JANET'S JOURNAL

Dear God,

Going through trials has always drawn us closer to You and each other. I have to admit in the midst of the problem, like each of us finding our space and our pace in this new living arrangement, we struggled until we took our eyes off what was bothering us about each other and looked to You for what was bothering You about our behavior.

We found ourselves apologizing and sitting down together to pray and work out a plan agreeable to each of us. Thank You, Lord, for being at the center of our lives and our marriage.

Drawing closer, Janet

A WIFE SHARES: *Carole Lewis* (FIRST PLACE 4 HEALTH)

In 1997, my husband, Johnny, was diagnosed with stage four prostate cancer with a prognosis of one to two years to live. Praise God he is still with me! My office has been at home for the last two years, and I absolutely love being with him all day. I work four hours in the morning and run downstairs to fix our lunch and clean up the mess in less than an hour. I go back to my office upstairs, but I'm close if he needs me.

We have learned so much about marriage since his diagnosis. I guess we both thought we would live to the age of 99 and die within days of each other! Cancer makes us appreciate every minute God gives us and not ever spend time angry.

Many women's husbands die suddenly and they don't even have time to say good-bye or make things right. This causes so much pain and guilt. I don't want to have one regret if Johnny goes first or I go first. When I'm away, we talk on the phone every few hours and always say, "I love you" when we hang up. We never miss kissing hello or good-bye.

This year we celebrated 53 years of marriage and we never dreamed we would make it to 50 after his diagnosis. Johnny's cancer, although terrible, has been a tool God has used to make us love each other even more than we did before.

MENTORING MOMENT

When Dave and I were dating, we took a class called Marriage Builders. Each meeting, the pastor who taught the course and later married Dave and me, would write *God* at the top of a whiteboard. Then forming a triangle, he drew a stick figure husband in one corner and a stick figure wife in the other. Next, he drew the lines connecting the triangle with God at the pinnacle. Then he explained that when the wife and husband were looking only at each other, they were the farthest apart.

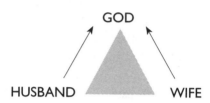

His point: every successful marriage has to have God as the head of the home. Each spouse draws closer to God and to each other as he or she works on an individual relationship with God. However, if one of them moves the focus away from God, they move back toward their respective corner, farther apart from God and each other.

Our marriages can survive having a stay-at-home man, but we don't want simply to *survive*, we want to *thrive!* Thriving hinges on our willingness to look at our own behavior and accept responsibility for areas *we* need to change while getting serious about our relationship with God.

- Have daily quiet times.
- Read God's Love Letter—the Bible.
- Pray alone and with your spouse.
- Ask others for prayer.
- Participate in a Bible study group or join one.
- Expect God to bless your marriage.
- Find creative ways to focus on the Lord, not circumstances.
- Pray both of you grows closer to God.
- If your spouse pulls away from God, stay strong in the Lord and pray your spouse follows suit. God will see you through this.

You might want to consult a *biblical* Christian marriage counselor to guide you as a couple through these uncharted waters. I emphasize *biblical* because God's Word is the only answer to the hope and peace you seek. Any other kind of counseling is simply someone's educated opinion, even from a Christian. When you learn how to glean wisdom and answers from your Bible, you may not need the counselor.

GOD'S **LOVE LETTER** TO YOU

*Dear*_____,

Draw near to Me with a sincere heart in full assurance of faith, having your hearts sprinkled to cleanse you from a guilty conscience, and having your bodies washed with pure water. Hold unswervingly to the hope you profess, for I who promised am faithful (Hebrews 10:22–23; paraphrased).

Closely, God

LET'S **PRAY**

Lord, we want to stay close to You so our hearts beat with Yours and we have the mind of Christ. When we're in tune with You, we'll be in perfect harmony with our husbands. Let us be a beacon of love drawing our husbands closer to You and to us. Guide us in how to lay down the life we once knew—selflessly and willingly. Only You know the number of our days—help us live our remaining earthly days in peace with our husbands. Amen.

YOUR LETTER TO GOD

Tell God how your faith has been tested and challenged. If your faith is shaky, ask God for a strengthening only He can provide.

Dear God,   *Date:*

_____

_____

_____

_____

_____

_____

FOR DISCUSSION

1. List ten ways you've seen God work in your marriage. How does this list help you rely on God in your current situation?

2. Do you pray together? If not, why not? What will you do to make this a spiritual habit?

3. How have you grown closer to God and to each other through this transition?

Chapter 13:

RESTORING THE JOY

I think we've adjusted well to being home together. I can truly say he is my best friend and he just happens to be my husband too!

— DEBBIE

Hallelujah!
Thank GOD! Pray to him by name!
Tell everyone you meet what he has done!
Sing him songs, belt out hymns,
*   translate his wonders into music!*
Honor his holy name with Hallelujahs,
*   you who seek GOD. Live a happy life!*

— PSALM 105:1–4 (*The Message*)

God will let you laugh again; you'll raise the roof with shouts of joy.   — JOB 8:21 (*The Message*)

Can I Get a Little Respect?
—or— Respect Is All He Needs!

I've learned to respect my husband's choices of where he's comfortable spending his time, and the best way to show him love is by making time for him.   — ALICE

However, each one of you also must love his wife as he loves himself, and the wife must respect her husband.   — EPHESIANS 5:33

JANET'S JOURNAL

Dear God,

I know how important it is for my actions and words to convey respect to Dave. I also know when I'm frustrated or upset—especially with our communication issues—I'm not always respectful. God, please help me express my feelings without crushing his spirit. He helps me so much with the ministry—I wouldn't be able to accomplish all that You've called me to do without his support and assistance. Help me show more appreciation and less criticism.

I must remember that he doesn't see things the same way I do and what bothers me, he may not even notice—and that's all right. Lord, You made us different, but You didn't intend for those differences to divide us.

Respectfully yours, Janet

A WIFE SHARES: *Joan*

After my retirement, I started speaking at women's retreats and teaching Precept Bible Studies. Harry and I were empty nesters and I loved the freedom—especially the peace and quiet to study and write for as long as I desired.

Every evening when Harry's huge imposing body filled the doorframe, my face lit up with joy! Then he decided to retire from his police lieutenant career. I was excited! What a great reward for his years of hard labor. We were both young—him 51 and me only 45. We looked forward to many years of joy doing things together!

Harry never regretted his decision to retire, and he quickly began investing time in his favorite hobbies . . . watching TV, Internet surfing, eating, and sleeping! *Joy* soon turned to *irritation* as a blaring TV or music filled my former quiet mornings. Where had my hours of peaceful contemplation of God's Word gone? Where had "my life" gone?

Even while reeling from shock at my drastically transformed life, I still had hopes we'd get into a natural rhythm and soon live in harmony. But months turned into years and nothing changed except me losing respect for my husband. I no longer lit up with delight when he walked through the door. I stopped listening carefully to or thinking very highly of his opinions.

I became the primary caretaker of bills, house cleaning, yard work, and my growing speaking ministry. In my mind, Harry didn't do enough to help, but actually made my life more difficult by not picking up after himself. When I'd return from speaking at weekend events to find his dishes, shoes, and socks strewn around the house, my heart sank with sadness and discouragement from feeling "put upon" and misunderstood. Why, if I worked so hard to make his life good, couldn't he help me—what else did he have to do?

A missionary friend came to stay with us and asked how Harry was doing with retirement. I said, "I'm worried about him. He's gained a lot of weight. He doesn't do much of anything but watch TV and surf the Net, and I don't think it's good for him. Will you pray for him?"

When I least expected it, God spoke in a powerful way through our humble friend. "Joan, I will pray. You're right, it probably isn't good for him; but no matter what he does, or doesn't do, respect your husband."

I was speechless and excused myself to my office. God had pointed out through our friend that I had lost respect for my husband. I was treating him like some unwelcome intruder in my life! I had sinned. I was to be my husband's helper, not him mine. I was to respect him, not for what he did or didn't do. I also realized having a husband who loved me dearly and treated me like pure gold was a great blessing.

In light of eternity . . . what are socks on the floor or plates piled high in the sink? Is having an orderly house worth making my husband miserable, and disappointing the Savior who died to make me free from the sin of selfishness? I'll answer to the Lord someday for my attitude toward my husband, not for the cleanliness of my house.

The Lord showed me that when I come home to a wonderfully quiet orderly house—just as I left it—is the day my precious giant will be at home with my Lord. It will be too late then to respect and love my husband. On that day, I would trade a clean house for more time with Harry.

When my husband walked through the door later that afternoon, my face again lit up with joy!

MENTORING MOMENT

I'm going to let Joan provide this mentoring moment. Her following points apply to any reason your man is home.

I've learned these things since Harry's been a stay-at-home man:
- Your husband hasn't infiltrated "your" territory. Your home is not *yours* alone, but a place of refuge for *both* of you. God made woman to be man's helpmate. Give your husband a place to enjoy life . . . you, family, and friends.

- Your goal is to have the happiest husband on earth—not the cleanest house on earth. It's OK to want a clean and orderly home, but it isn't OK to demand your requirements be met, "or else."
- Make your desires known prayerfully and humbly—not with disgust or demanding. Explain how much his compliance would mean to you. For example, I said to Harry, "I spend hours of my valuable time getting my heart right with the Lord so I can respect and love you as unto the Lord, whether or not you ever pick up after yourself! Please help me in my walk with Jesus by helping me at home—that's *your* responsibility." Slowly my husband responded. Now coming home from speaking is a treat!
- Husbands don't usually do things on purpose to irritate us. I used to think Harry did, but the truth is, he honestly doesn't care about the house. I had to convey in a loving and honest way that loving me means caring about things that bother me.
- Stick to the facts. Be patient. Improvement takes time.
- We are to build God's kingdom and serve Him, not build our kingdom and have our husbands serve us.
- The difficult years following a husband coming home should make you more Christlike, not more miserable. Use this trial to "*let patience have its perfect work, that you may be perfect and complete, lacking nothing*" (James 1:4 NKJV).

GOD'S **LOVE LETTER** TO YOU

Dear _____,

    "*A new command I give you: Love one another. As I have loved you, so you must love one another*" (John 13:34).

Respectfully, God

LET'S **PRAY**

Abba, Father. Our husbands need our respect—especially those husbands who aren't feeling worthy or valuable right now. Please give us words to build them up, not tear them down. Help us see our husbands as You do—worthy of love and respect. Amen.

Please Change Him — I Mean Me

I was convinced I had huge problems, but it wasn't all Harry. Continually I prayed, asking God how I could change my strained marriage, how I could change my hard heart, and how I could put back together what was broken. And God answered. My husband didn't change as much as I did! —JOAN

The Lord your God will change your heart and the hearts of all your descendants, so that you will love him with all your heart and soul and so you may live! —DEUTERONOMY 30:6 (NLT)

JANET'S JOURNAL

Dear God,

You would think that after 20 years of marriage, I'd realize my husband isn't going to change in all the ways I want him to . . . and he's probably wishing I would change too . . . or maybe I have changed in ways he wishes I hadn't!

I can only change me and pray Dave will respond in a way that pleases us both. Lord, You are always pointing out to me the need to be humble and to set my "needs" aside for the greater good of our marriage and our witness to other couples. It seems like I need a daily reminder.

Help me to recognize and praise the things about Dave that are honorable and warm my heart, and let me unload at Your feet the things that burden me. Lord, please guide me in how to discuss hurtful issues with him in a way he'll receive and not become defensive or shut down. Change my heart, Lord, and renew my mind.

Changing, Janet

A WIFE SHARES: Heather

I had been praying for God to change my husband's negative attitude. I was frustrated and didn't know what to do. As I prayed, God spoke lovingly that I should pray for *my* attitude first. I began praying for God to change me: I would cease seeking praise from my husband, but would work to honor God. I prayed God would use me to build up my husband and never stop blessing him, regardless of his reactions. Instead of praying for *his* attitude to change, I prayed he would receive honor and respect at work, our children would see him as the wonderful man he is, and he would be encouraged and refreshed when home.

Serving God, not man, restores my heart. It's a blessing to everyone when our priorities are set straight. My husband has been pouring out love and help in ways I haven't seen in a very long time. He is showing a loving and caring side I don't often see from my not-so-emotional, engineer-minded man. My renewed and strengthened marriage honors God.

I will love my husband no matter what, but lately, I've had a smile that won't fade. I'm so thankful God showed me the way He desires, not what I thought should happen!

(Note: Heather's husband is not a stay-at-home man yet, but I love how her change of heart changed her husband.)

MENTORING MOMENT

In *Why Can't HE Be More Like ME?*, Poppy Smith advises wives to accept our husbands just the way God made them:

> Most women expect acceptance and love from their husbands. Ironically, many wives find it hard to give acceptance and love in turn, especially if their spouse fails to live up to their expectations. In response to their feelings of frustration, many embark on a spousal remodeling project, but they rarely succeed. No matter how hard wives try to change their husbands, few men are willing to let them succeed.

All of us could compose a list of things we would like to change about our husbands and they could do likewise—although I think we would agree that wives tend to be greater change agents than husbands. I hope just as quickly, we could come up with an even longer list of the things—yes, even the quirks—we love about our husbands.

Then there's the list of changes *we* need to make—not for the purpose of the resultant change in our husbands—but because we want to be godly women whose hearts are right with God. Let's start with that list.

As Heather experienced in the above "A Wife Shares," there's a good chance that as we change, we'll observe some of the changes we're longing for in our husbands. Even if this doesn't happen for a very long time, in the process we'll become women pleasing to God—what husband could resist!

GOD'S **LOVE LETTER** TO YOU

Dear_____,

A change of heart is produced by God's Spirit. And a person with a changed heart seeks praise from Me, God, not from people (Romans 2:29 NLT; paraphrased).

Your Change Agent, God

LET'S **PRAY**

O Lord, change our hearts—make them true. Humble us and remove the pride that so easily entangles us and causes us to look at others as less worthy than ourselves. Give us a quiet and gentle spirit and words that edify and build up, not destroy and tear down. Restore to us the joy of our early years of marriage—even when circumstances are not of our choosing. Amen.

Can You Hear Him Now?

Two-way communication involves the art of listening, always subject to interpretation. —JOSEPH

He who answers before listening—that is his folly and his shame.
—PROVERBS 18:13

JANET'S **JOURNAL**

Dear God,

You know Dave's and my differing communication styles have been the source of either hilarious or hysterical interaction since the day we met. Soon after our honeymoon, I bought Bible studies on communication for us to do together . . . we read books . . . we discussed the problem exhaustively . . . but communication remains our primary unresolved issue. Being home together 24/7 only escalates this ongoing problem.

My biggest complaint is Dave not hearing me, which I perceive as: he's not listening. I even made him have a hearing test, but except for high tones, his hearing is excellent. I feel rejected and ignored when he doesn't answer a question or respond to a comment, and irritated when his comeback is, "What?" Lord, communication is essential for relationships and miscommunication severely taxes ours.

Recently when I was doing a book signing at a local Christian bookstore, Dave picked up the book *How to Get Your Husband to Listen to You.* I realized two things: Dave really did want to help solve this problem, and other women have the same problem.

Is it possible that because Dave's around all the time now, I'm talking to him more about things he doesn't relate to and in ways he doesn't receive? Wow! We have a great deal of work to do in this area, but I think we've made a breakthrough.

Listening and learning, Janet

A WIFE SHARES: *Sharron*

If my husband were not my husband, I would want him to be my husband. I like him as a friend and love him as my lifemate. What a surprise when he retired and we were together 24/7 . . . a little thing I loved about him turned into a big thing that irritated me.

He was doing what he'd always done, offering reminders I appreciated. As I walked out the door to run to the market, "Honey, did you remember your list?" Getting ready for bed, "Do you remember your dentist appointment tomorrow morning?" But his continual reminders slowly became irritating and I started to think, *What does he think, I'm an idiot?*

Was it him or me? The easy answer was, "It's him!" So I took it to God, "Do you see what he's doing?"

Wanting to hear from God was a good place to start. I began to see it was me . . . yes, *moi!* I was the one with the *attitude.* I had a glimpse of life without my husband—how much I'd miss his friendship and *those* reminders. God opened my eyes and allowed me to see my husband's heart. What a kindness not to let me get to the store and then realize I didn't have my list. I have forgotten my dentist appointment and he knows how important it is to me not to do that again.

I asked God to forgive me. I asked Him to give me a heart of gratitude for a husband who cared enough to remind me. I prayed God would bless him for loving me the way he does.

Whenever I hear, "Are you remembering . . . ?" It reminds me how pride gets in our way. I didn't like what my aging mind was doing and my husband's reminders made me look squarely at something I wanted to ignore. I now see him as God's agent helping me acknowledge what I was trying to avoid. I've since embraced the changes that come with age. With an appreciative heart, I tell my husband the truth, "I was forgetting . . . thank you for the reminder . . . babe!"

JANET'S PS: When I lived in California, Sharron and I walked together almost every morning. After her husband retired, he decided he was going to walk with us. We wondered how this would affect our girl talk, but he fell in right behind us and we kept walking and talking like usual. Then one morning when he had to get to a meeting, we looked up from our conversation to see he had passed us and was quickly out of sight. Soon it was just Sharron and me walking and talking again.

MENTORING MOMENT

When you're around each other 24/7, little things you ignored in the past or "put up with" can now become landmines waiting detonation by one misspoken word or irritating habit. For me the landmine was not feeling heard. This always bothered me, but miscommunication *all* day, *every* day, creates constant tension.

Find an *appropriate* time to sit down with your husband face-to-face and express your thoughts and concerns about an annoying behavior or attitude. Use kind and loving words. Avoid "you always" or "you never" comments and deal with one issue at a time—don't verbally assault him with *every* irritating thing he's done since being home. Timing and tone are everything.

Anita said when her husband first retired from his suit and tie career, he also retired from daily hygiene and putting on clean clothes! When she brought this to his attention, he replied he wasn't going anywhere so why clean up. She kindly told him that *she* was the reason. An aha moment for him.

I wonder if creating differing male and female communication styles and thought processes was God's plan to get us to work harder at dying to our impatient and intolerant pride: the need to be heard, understood, and right. A lifetime may not be long enough to be a student of your mate, but God has brought the two of you together for a reason, and it may take a lifetime to figure out why. So don't waste the time you have together not hearing each other—listen for God's still, small voice and ask Him to help you communicate joyfully—not jeeringly. It will make a world of difference—one word at a time.

GOD'S **LOVE LETTER** TO YOU

*Dear*_____,

   "My dear brothers [and sisters], take note of this: Everyone should be quick to listen, slow to speak and slow to become angry" (James 1:19).
                                        Listening, God

LET'S **PRAY**

Lord, we want to laugh more and criticize less. Help us speak clearly and in love to our husbands and listen to his heart's intentions when he speaks. Give us wisdom and discernment every time we open our mouths and give us ears to hear You, and our husbands, clearly. Amen.

Rejoicing in and Through the Trials

As I looked for God at work in our daily lives, my perspective began to change.   — CHAR

Keep your eyes open for GOD, watch for his works; be alert for signs of his presence.   — PSALM 105:4 (*The Message*)

JANET'S JOURNAL

Dear God,

Dave's and my goal and constant desire is to be role models and mentors of how a Christian marriage weathers the storms of life. You inspired us to design our wedding invitation with the image of a cross and three chords braided around it. We also included Psalm 126:3, *"The Lord has done great things for us and we are filled with joy,"* and Ecclesiastes 4:12, *"A cord of three strands is not quickly broken."*

The invitation read: "Each of us alone is incomplete, together with Christ we are as one, and believing this, Janet Hollinger and David Thompson invite you to share in our joy as we come united in Christian marriage and place our lives in the Lord's hands."

Unsure of what lay ahead in blending two families who had experienced divorce, we knew that with Your Son, Jesus Christ, at the center of our marriage, we could withstand anything the world threw at us. And so far, we have.

When we moved to Idaho, we were the "new kids on the mountain." Obviously Your plan, but unbeknown to us, we discovered we were living in an area with many stay-at-home husbands and wives who mentored us in living in this rural area. You knew just what we needed—thank You!

We've always been open about how You've seen us through struggles. We pray that as we continue adapting to this new season of life, You'll use us as You've done in the past to help others see that having a relationship with You is the only way to *grow*, and not simply *go*, through trials and transitions. We give You all the glory for the things You have done.

Mentoring, Janet

A WIFE SHARES: *Vanessa*

Today, I say, "Dear God, thank You, he's home!" And, "Thank You, he's my best friend," because we spend lots of time together waiting for my husband's kidney transplant and dealing with all my issues from the horrific bicycle accident.

With our respective disabilities, it's a challenge for us to balance needed rest, ministry, time together, time alone with God, and proper exercise. Usually our time together doesn't suffer. I try to go with him to his church ministry meetings and he's helped me volunteer at Christian writers' conferences. We take walks around our neighborhood and go to the gym together.

When my writing inordinately envelopes me, Greg gets my attention by singing with his lovely baritone voice. I think, *It's time to get up, take a break, and stretch or I won't be able to move these stiffening joints at all!* Greg wanting my attention blesses me.

We each have good and bad days with our health. On our good days, we get so excited we need boundaries not to overdo. I need to watch my crankiness when my symptoms flair up and not snap at the one closest to me. When we're both feeling down, it's a good time to take catnaps and catch up on doing laundry together.

God works our tribulations together for good. The guy I met 12 and a half years ago, after praying for God to bring the "strand of love" into my life from Ecclesiastes 4:12 — *"A cord of three strands is not quickly broken."* —remains the strand I'd prayed for: *Jesus, my husband, and me.*

MENTORING MOMENT

Challenging times transform our character: We develop a deeper level of maturity and understanding of God, others, and ourselves. Don't worry if it's too soon to think positively about your life adjustments. When the time is right, reread this book. Let the stories of God, turning everything for good in a believer's life and marriage, restore and renew your hope.

Maybe you're ready to admit: Lord, I wouldn't have chosen this path for us right now, but thank You for the ways You've used it to mold and make us more like You. Every wife of a stay-at-home man who surrendered her will to God's will realized a purpose in the transitions and rediscovered joy in her marriage and relationship with God.

GOD'S LOVE LETTER TO YOU

Dear_____,

"Dear brothers and sisters, when troubles come your way, consider it an opportunity for great joy. For you know that when your faith is tested, your endurance has a chance to grow. So let it grow, for when your endurance is

fully developed, you will be perfect and complete, needing nothing" (James 1:2–4 NLT).

Rejoicing, God

LET'S **PRAY**

Lord, we don't like trials and tribulations and try our best to avoid them, but we can't change our current circumstances. Guide us in using our trials for Your glory. Help us remember all the promises in the Bible and look for the good You'll bring out of difficult times. We know others are watching and we want to be a good witness that when You're at the center of our lives and marriages, all things are possible—even the seemingly impossible. Amen.

YOUR LETTER TO GOD

Ask God to remind you of something that puts a smile on your face, restores joy, and shows you the light at the end of the tunnel.

Dear God,   *Date:*

_____

_____

_____

_____

_____

_____

_____

_____

_____

_____

_____

_____

_____

_____

_____

_____

FOR **DISCUSSION**

1. Where have you been disrespectful to each other and how could you rectify your behavior?

2. How has your heart changed since starting this book?

3. What steps could you take (or have you taken) to restore or renew joy in your marriage?

Chapter 14:
ENDING AT THE BEGINNING

I cling to believing there's a reason for things happening, and in the wake of loss, there's a context for a new beginning.　　— CHERI

And the one sitting on the throne said, "Look, I am making all things new!" And then he said to me, "Write this down, for what I tell you is trustworthy and true." And he also said, "It is finished! I am the Alpha and the Omega—the Beginning and the End. To all who are thirsty I will give the springs of the water of life without charge!"　　— REVELATION 21:5–6 (NLT)

Begin with Gratitude for Unexpected Blessings

One of the biggest blessings of changing roles is my husband having dinner ready for me when I come home from teaching on my "long day" at 10:00 P.M.　　— VEOLA

When my husband retired, in some ways the laundry got bigger but it also got smaller—it was a blessing not washing and ironing all those white shirts!　　— ROSEMARY

Rather than add up my complaints, I simply relish my many, often continuous, blessings.　　— JOSEPH

GOD made my life complete when I placed all the pieces before him. When I got my act together, he gave me a fresh start. Now I'm alert to GOD's ways; I don't take God for granted. Every day I review the ways he works; I try not to miss a trick. I feel put back together, and I'm watching my step. GOD rewrote the text of my life when I opened the book of my heart to his eyes.

　　— PSALM 18:20–24 *(The Message)*

JANET'S JOURNAL

Dear God,

Each time Dave has been "home," You've used it for good. During his first layoff, he taught me how to compose and write on the computer, and I wrote the *Woman to Woman Mentoring* resources. His second layoff coincided with my first breast cancer battle so he was able to care for me and go to doctor's visits.

In this retirement season, he has essentially become my assistant for About His Work Ministries. Over the years, I've pleaded and prayed for an assistant, but Lord, I never thought it would be *Dave.* You've gifted him with technical and electronic skills to complement my creative writing and business skills. Having him available 24/7, and not just in the evenings after a long day at work or on weekends, has helped us advance the ministry in ways I could never do on my own.

We're learning so much about our relationship, our ministry, and ourselves. It's such a blessing to be free to travel and visit our grandchildren and children scattered throughout the country and be available when they need our help and support.

I didn't see this season coming and wasn't ready to succumb to it, but I do see how You're using the time we have left together to enrich our lives, as well as the lives of others.

Blessed, Janet

A WIFE SHARES: *Deb*

When my husband "retired" several years ago, I wasn't worried. He was a high-powered executive, and I assumed he'd be back to work within six months. Was I wrong!

The first thing he did was turn his highly astute financial eye on our finances! Understand I'd been doing the bookkeeping and paying the bills for the past 20-odd years. Suddenly, he's questioning me. I was highly offended but had learned *not* to express those feelings verbally.

I thought and prayed about it—for at least a week. The answer was simple: Give him access to the online bank account and credit cards. He could see what bills came in and how I paid them. He would realize why we "never had the money" he thought we did and would compliment me on how well I'd handled things.

The result wasn't what I'd anticipated—no compliments, to my dismay. He now wanted to know why we spent the money we did—and he saw how much online shopping I do! After much discussion, we arrived at an amiable solution: He tracks all our expenses in his program and lets me know when it's OK to spend or when I need to be frugal. He now sees that "emergencies" come up on a regular basis. We still have stress over finances, but it doesn't stress our relationship.

As we've been together more the last few years, he sees "what I do all day" and how I arrange my time. He has time to watch TV—all the talking heads and anything involving a ball. I have time to play my computer games and talk with friends. We've learned to do things together and to care for each other more. What could have been a disaster has become one of my greatest blessings!

MENTORING MOMENT

Many wives referred to their journey of adjusting to a stay-at-home man as a blessing and a gift as they discovered the wisdom and reasons behind God's perfect plan and timing. Most agreed this experience changed their lives and their marriages for the better once they released their "issues" to God. That might be difficult to consider right now. It was tough for them too in the beginning, just as it was for Dave and me. But when God's plan began unfolding, we all finally appreciated why He had us on this journey.

Have you had difficulty rejoicing and finding blessings in your husband being a stay-at-home man? Do the hardships of this transition far outweigh the blessings at this point? If so, I understand, and so does God. Pray for comfort the world cannot give. Let God wrap His arms around your heart and cheer you up.

As blessings begin to unveil, and they will or maybe they have already, thank God and write them down so you remember His faithfulness. In "Sanity Tools," page 186, you'll find "I Am So Happy Because . . . ". It's a place to linger and count your blessings. Alice said she started a gratitude journal that's brought her peace and a renewed appreciation for her husband.

If you have trouble getting started, list all the things you love about your husband and why you're grateful God brought him into your life.

As you write, your heart will begin singing. On difficult days, read what you wrote. I love this quote from Hannah Moore: "When thou hast truly thanked the Lord for every blessing sent, but little time will then remain for murmur or lament."

GOD'S **LOVE LETTER** TO YOU

*Dear*_____,

"My thoughts are nothing like your thoughts," says the LORD. *"And my ways are far beyond anything you could imagine. For just as the heavens are higher than the earth, so my ways are higher than your ways and my thoughts higher than your thoughts. It is the same with my word. I send it out, and it always produces fruit. It will accomplish all I want it to, and it will prosper everywhere I send it. You will live in joy and peace. The mountains and hills will burst into song, and the trees of the field will clap their hands!"* (Isaiah 55:8–9, 11–12 NLT).

Abundant Blessings, God

LET'S **PRAY**

Lord, transform us and make us into the women You designed us to be. We might not have chosen this journey, but since we're on it, please help us acknowledge the blessings along the way and become better wives to our husbands so they feel blessed too. Amen.

Making Your Story Your Testimony

God can take your mess and create His success. — MONA

A changed life coupled to a clear testimony will attract people to Jesus; and in the end, that's what our Christian life is all about.

— PASTOR TIM WESTCOTT

Generation after generation stands in awe of your work; each one tells stories of your mighty acts. — PSALM 145:4 (*The Message*)

JANET'S JOURNAL

Dear God,

Our family and friends joke: "Be careful what you tell Mom/Janet or it'll end up in her next book!" I always tell people going through a challenging time to keep a journal because You're going to make their struggle their testimony. Making *our* story—*Your* Story—provides perspective and a witness.

God, if You're going to use Dave's and my testimony to help others, we must be open, vulnerable, and honest. When I shared with Dave my desire to write this book, he knew our lives would become an "open book." Thank You, Lord, for Dave's willingness to share our story to help other couples—a testimony in itself.

Testifying, Janet

A WIFE SHARES: *Char*

"Hi, honey!" Richard rose from the piano keyboard as I entered the house, my arms full of groceries. "I got the offer! I start 40 hours per week on July 1. Want to go out and celebrate?"

I felt a spontaneous pang of disappointment, but quickly corrected myself. *This is what you've been praying about for the past 32 months. Of course we should celebrate!*

"That's wonderful, honey." I gave him a one-arm hug. "Sure. Let me set these things down and we can be on our way."

Over dinner at our favorite health-food restaurant, we reflected on the various stages of answered prayer during Richard's unemployment. We had a lot to be thankful for, but I couldn't shake my first reaction: Disappointed? It begged the question, *What did I expect from God anyway? What was my gut-level spontaneous reaction trying to tell me?*

I should have been thrilled. The waiting, the anxieties . . . over. But by the time Richard got this offer, his lack of full-time work had ceased to matter. With my work and Richard's two part-time positions, we were meeting our financial obligations and had stopped drawing down our savings. I was enjoying renewed career success. Our son John had earned a full-fees scholarship to his chosen university. We had abundant blessings.

What I'd failed to take into consideration while waiting for Richard's perfect job offer was that God wanted to do something big for *everyone* in our family—not just for Richard. All of us now had perfect jobs according to God's plan and of His choosing.

What had I *really* wanted from God? I wanted security—free of worrying about money. Long before the perfect job presented itself, God had already met my needs—even the ones I didn't know I had! I need to share this with others in a similar situation—it's our testimony.

MENTORING MOMENT

The purpose of the women and men in this book voicing their struggles and victories was to offer you hope, guidance, and encouragement. Each *story* became a *testimony* when God received the glory—the focus shifted from personal pain to God's gain—regardless of how the story ended.

Those who share their stories, including Dave and I, will never forget the glorious work of the Lord because we have it in writing. If you haven't been journaling in the space provided, go back now and write your letters to God, and use "Prayer and Praise Journal," page 187. Your faith will strengthen as you see the mighty hand of the Lord in your life. Circumstances aren't just random happenings. When there seems to be no way, God *always* makes a way—His way.

Maybe you've heard: *Make your mess your message.* You can be sure God will bring into your life a woman struggling with a stay-at-home man, and He's going to ask you to reach out to her and share what helped you make it through your tough times—and you will—right? When you're ready, God will use your testimony to change lives—starting with your own.

GOD'S LOVE LETTER TO YOU

Dear_____,

You're here to be light, bringing out the God-colors in the world. I, God, am not a secret to be kept. We're going public with this, as public as a city on a hill. If I make you light-bearers, you don't think I'm going to hide you under a bucket, do you? I'm putting you on a light stand. Now that I've put you there on a hilltop, on a light stand—shine! Keep open house; be generous with your lives. By opening up to others, you'll prompt people to open up with Me, God, a generous Father in heaven (Matthew 5:14–16 The Message; paraphrased).

Giving You a Testimony, God

LET'S **PRAY**

Father, it's hard to imagine how You could use our ordinary stories to make a difference in another woman's life. Sometimes we just want to keep our situation to ourselves . . . it's so private and personal. . . . But if You think we could help another woman, we're willing to pray with her, share our story, and help her turn her thoughts and actions over to You. Use us if You will and help us make *our* story *Your* story. Amen.

We've Only Just Begun!

The children are grown, so we talk more now. We can enjoy our time on the porch or in our rocking chairs—together.

— ZELMYRA, MARRIED 86 YEARS

Remember the former things, those of long ago; I am God, and there is no other; I am God, and there is none like me. I make known the end from the beginning, from ancient times, what is still to come. I say: My purpose will stand, and I will do all that I please.   —ISAIAH 46:9–10

JANET'S **JOURNAL**

Dear God,

When Dave and I married, I saw it as the end of looking for Mr. Right in all the wrong places and an opportunity for a new beginning—the end of 17 years as a single mom—the beginning of a second chance at having a good marriage. And what would make it good? Well, not Dave's job, his income potential, the security he offered, or his good looks. No, those could all disappear in a heartbeat—and they did, except for his good looks. Dave *was* Mr. Right because he is a righteous man who loves You, God, more than he loves me.

Lord, You gave me the godly man I'd been searching for and I was so grateful to You for bringing him into my life. Then, I started taking him for granted—feeling too deserving and entitled. As life "happened," I realized we would continue going through a multitude of endings and beginnings until we finally reach the ultimate new beginning in heaven with You. In the process, I hope to die to my own fleshly desires and prideful "rights" and display more of Your thoughts, emotions, and insights toward Dave.

Thank You for giving Dave patience with me. Not that I have this all figured out or have "arrived" as a wife, but I have my eyes on You as I try to be a role model for others to follow. I hope You will say to me someday, "You became the 'wiffy' I made you to be." Well done!

Continually evolving, Janet

A WIFE SHARES: *Karen O'Connor*

Here we are 12 years since Charles retired and we're doing just fine. After his "official retirement," he took a part-time job as a tour guide for a local company, which occupied a couple of days a week for about four years. He was happy with the diversion and I was ecstatic to have the house to myself on those days.

However, that routine ended when we moved to a new city to be near one of our daughters and grandchildren. Charles decided then, at age 76, he *really* would retire from any kind of employment except puttering in our garden, doing the laundry, shuttling the grandkids around, and cooking an occasional meal.

We've been settled into this "new" phase of life for five years now, and it's filled with blessings—time together at the gym, in the kitchen, on the sofa watching the evening news, walking along the beach, at church, enjoying the symphony on Sunday afternoons, and visiting our family nearby—without the concern for having to "be at work."

We've renewed our friendship as well as our marriage—and I still meet all my writing deadlines. Each day Charles wakes up and starts singing in his beautiful tenor voice and one of the first questions he asks is, "What can I do to make your day easier?"

That question alone is definitely a step in the right direction!

(Note: Karen O'Connor is the author of a series of books on growing older. Look for more information under "Books and Resources," p. 178.)

MENTORING MOMENT

Wherever you are on the journey with your stay-at-home man—just beginning, feeling stuck in the middle, seeing your dreams fulfilled, or following a new dream—God is working on a parallel dream bigger than you can imagine. It's never just about you; it's always about God's purpose of furthering His kingdom here on earth and taking care of *all* His children. He wants you to help Him fulfill His vision while He works on helping you fulfill your dreams.

Jesus' death on the Cross wasn't the end of the story God is writing. The Cross was just the beginning, and because Jesus trusted God— *"Yet I want your will to be done, not mine"* (Mark 14:36 NLT)—you and I have the opportunity to end our old sinful life and begin a new life in Christ. If you or your husband haven't made a commitment to follow Jesus, why not take that new beginning step right now! Go to page 174 and pray the new beginning prayer.

The end of one journey is the beginning of the next adventure. With God in your life, He promises to bring good out of whatever you're going through (Romans 8:28). Trust God for your new beginning:

> The things that began to happen after that were so great and beautiful that I cannot write them. And for us this is the end of all the stories, and we can most truly say that they all lived happily ever after. But for them it was only the beginning of the real story. All their life in this world and all their adventures in Narnia had only been the cover and the title page; now at last they were beginning Chapter One of the Great Story which no one on earth has read, which goes on forever, in which every chapter is better than the one before.
>
> —C. S. Lewis (*The Last Battle*)

GOD'S **LOVE LETTER** TO YOU

Dear _____,

My dear friends, I'm not writing anything new here. This is the oldest commandment in my book, and you've known it from day one. It's always been implicit in the Message you've heard from me. On the other hand, perhaps it is new, freshly minted as it is in both Christ and you—the darkness on its way out and the True Light already blazing! (1 John 2:7–8 *The Message*; paraphrased).

> *I AM the Alpha and the Omega, the Beginning and the End, the New Beginning, God*

LET'S **PRAY**

Lord, starting over or going into something new isn't easy. Sometimes we stubbornly hold onto the known and resist the wonder of a new life adventure. Regardless of why our man is home, life will be different, but it doesn't have to be distressing. Give us the tools and desire to make the rest of our life together the best. Amen.

We Will Never Be the Same Again —or—It's All About Love!

L-isten, O-verlook faults, V-oice approval, E-ffort = LOVE — ANITA

It will never be the same again. — EZEKIEL 7:13 (*The Message*)

JANET'S **JOURNAL**

Dear God,

Life is different now, and most of the time that's a good thing. Lord, over the years You have provided for us financially, given us a comfortable home and an incredible community of friends and church family, both in California and Idaho. Our four amazing children and their spouses all know You as their personal Savior—what a blessing. Our young grandchildren are starting to make commitments to Your Son, Jesus Christ—what a legacy. Really, could it get any better this side of heaven?

Going forward, I want everyone in our life to know how much I love my stay-at-home man and what a gift from You he is to me. And for our friends and family to say about us: The Thompsons—our friends—our neighbors—our parents—Grammie and Grampa Dave—love the Lord and love each other.

Lovingly, Janet

TWO WIVES **SHARE:** *Elizabeth*

It's been wonderful this past 14 months having my husband of 40 years working away on his freelance architecture projects in the room above my office. We email each other about lunch, who's cooking dinner, or where we should take our walk. It's like dating again.

However, having a husband home 24/7 isn't all bliss. As an interior designer, I like my house photo-ready. It's hard sometimes, as he has taken over the guest room *and* the dining room table to lay out the huge sets of drawings he needs to review. But for social events, he picks up and assists with the heavy cleaning. I respect his need for space and he respects my need to socialize.

You cannot go into this transition of having a full-time, in-home husband thinking your life will be the same: Consideration, communication, and a positive attitude are essential for adapting. I'm not nearly as productive. Lunchtime used to be all of 15 minutes eaten in front of my computer as I scanned the news of the day—now it can be an hour or more. My exercise time was 45 minutes and now it can be two hours if we take a long hike.

At times, this lack of production frustrates my achievement-driven personality. I remind myself we're making precious memories together. We will never have this hour, this day, or this month again. Many of my friends are already widows.

Over the years, my husband has ventured into the kitchen and tried cooking. We now share the cooking responsibilities based on who is the busiest or who wants to cook. Often we prepare a meal together, talking our way through: "I'm chopping the onions. Do you want to do the carrots?" With lots of communication, we're able to work together.

Remember getting married—the desire to be always with your spouse? Have you maintained those feelings throughout your marriage? You probably became busy with careers and kids. *Now* is the time to enjoy being together.

Linda

Chuck and I have been happily married for 44 years, and like many couples, we've had our share of ups and downs. But we're honestly at a place today where we both can say we're more in love than we've ever been. And the good news is my husband works from home! My mother-in-law always said, "For better or worse, but not for lunch." Well, I have a different perspective.

My husband has worked very hard, including seven different career changes, to provide us with a good life and many blessings—but it came with a cost. He was mostly in full-commission sales and worked nights and weekends. Thank God, he didn't have to travel, but I always wanted more time with him between raising a family, church involvement, extended family, and friends.

So for me, having him working out of our home is a dream come true. I love when his flexible schedule allows us to have breakfast and lunch together or go out for lunch, do devotions and Bible study together, or share frequent walks and grandparenting. He's also helpful with household tasks. Our time together is so much more than ever before. I'm truly blessed. The best is yet to come!

MENTORING MOMENT

Reality check—he's home! Our best recourse is to do everything we can to make the transition as smooth and positive as possible. We've talked about many ideas and suggestions in this book, and other wives have shared with you what worked and didn't work for them. I'm sure you had numerous aha moments, as did I, where you identified with the wife sharing or you saw a new way to look at your situation.

Life is about growing and maturing spiritually, physically, emotionally, mentally, and relationally. The Bible tells us in 1 Corinthians 13:11 that when we were children we talked, thought, reasoned, and acted like children; but now we're grown up and we need to put away our childish ways:
• Wanting things our *own* way
• Considering only *our* needs
• Quarreling
• Throwing fits and having meltdowns
• Not taking no for an answer
And put on our wifely ways:
• Wanting things that are best for *both* of us
• Considering *both* our needs
• Peacemaking
• Acting rationally
• Accepting no as an answer
If you're like me, the older I get, the better I "get it"!

GOD'S **LOVE LETTER** TO YOU

*Dear*_____ ,

"*Love is patient, love is kind. It does not envy, it does not boast, it is not proud. It is not rude, it is not self-seeking, it is not easily angered, it keeps no record of wrongs. Love does not delight in evil but rejoices with the truth. It always protects, always trusts, always hopes, always perseveres*" (1 Corinthians 13:4–7).

Love Always, God

LET'S **PRAY**

Heavenly Father, we can't imagine the infinite love You have for us. Teach us to love our husbands with unconditional love. Help us accept the things we cannot change from the past and have a positive attitude about our future. We know we can do all things through Your Son, Jesus Christ, the source of our strength and endurance. We love You, Lord, and we love our husbands. Help us make our homes heaven on earth for our stay-at-home man. Amen.

YOUR **LETTER** TO GOD

Talk with God about a new beginning in your marriage. If you're ready to start a new life in Christ, go now to the new beginning prayer on page 174.

Dear God,   *Date:*

_____

_____

_____

_____

_____

_____

_____

_____

_____

_____

_____

FOR **DISCUSSION**

1. Share unexpected blessings you've experienced with your husband being home.

2. What elements of your story could become your testimony and where could you share it?

3. What new beginning is God starting in your marriage?

My New Beginning Prayer

And this is the plan: At the right time he will bring everything together under the authority of Christ—everything in heaven and on earth. Furthermore, because of Christ, we have received an inheritance from God, for he chose us from the beginning, and all things happen just as he decided long ago. —EPHESIANS 1:10–11 (NLT)

Dear God,

I believe You sent Your Son, Jesus, to die on a cross and rise to life three days later to wipe away my sins and give me eternal life with You. I know I have sinned, and I ask for Your forgiveness. I don't understand everything about being a Christian, and I still have some questions; but I do know I want to accept Your invitation to come into my heart, and I'm willing to learn more about what that means. Thank You for offering me the gift of salvation. In Jesus' name, I pray. Amen.

Congratulations! You accepted Jesus into your heart as your personal Savior. Welcome to the family of God.

EPILOGUE

MY STAY-AT-HOME MAN SHARES

Throughout our marriage and my professional career, God has provided windows into life as a stay-at-home man—temporary times of unemployment, working out of my home office, and various careers. My last job was physically demanding and eventually led to reconstructive foot surgery, which resulted in an unexpected medical retirement and becoming a full-time stay-at-home man.

Our life as we knew it changed dramatically in six months: I went from planning to work until I was 67 to a medical disability at 64½ and retiring early at 65.

I couldn't have imagined what God had planned for us, but He orchestrated everything and His timing was perfect. He thought of every little detail like coordinating the exact timing of my job termination with my 65th birthday and eligibility for Medicare and providing COBRA insurance for Janet until her 65th birthday. Because of Janet's history of breast cancer, she would have been uninsurable without an employer group policy and I was now unable to work. God is good!

I rapidly determined retirement wasn't feasible where we lived in Southern California. Then God opened the door for us to move to the mountains where we had always wanted to live and retire—just not in our cabin in the Idyllwild, California, mountains, but in the Garden Valley, Idaho, mountains where we could enjoy a more fulfilling life, which I dearly love.

Still, retirement created challenges in our relationship, as Janet related in our story. Living together 24/7 has probably been the biggest adjustment and my realizing Janet's serious need for space and dedicated writing time. Communication patterns and some of my priorities had to change! We had to develop a plan for communication and sharing household responsibilities.

I also went from a maintenance-free yard with a gardener in California to now having almost an acre of land to maintain, which has worked out fine with Janet wanting isolation while writing. However, this city boy had a lot to learn about the wilderness and maintaining a mountain home. It's been fun and I'm still learning. I wouldn't change our life now for anything other than God calling us somewhere else.

As Janet says, I took to this season as if I'd been working for it all my life. No kidding, I *had been* working my entire career to enjoy the finer things of life! I'm embracing retirement and love our small mountain community with the beauty of God's creation literally right outside our door. We're surrounded by mountains, pine trees, rushing rivers, forests, lakes and nature, and oh yes, *no* traffic! I wake up in the morning to deer sauntering around our property, watching elk on the mountain behind our home and in the meadows, dodging an occasional bear, feeding birds, and slowing down our pace of life.

I have more time to help with About His Work Ministries, serve at church, read, draw nearer to the Lord, spend time with family, enjoy being Grampa Dave to our 11 wonderful grandchildren, travel to see our kids, watch grandkids' soccer and baseball games, plant and maintain a vegetable and herb garden, play my guitar, . . . and, oh yes . . . play more golf!

So I leave you with these final words: Living with your spouse in stay-at-home man seasons of life, while different, is no more challenging than any other season of married life. You just have to constantly die to self as God teaches us, consider your spouse more important than yourself, and work as a team. I like the wise council I gleaned from Promise Keepers years ago and ultimately conveyed to my son, sons-in-law, and men's small-group studies—marriage isn't a 50/50 proposition as proposed by some, but 100/0. If you give 100 percent and expect zero in return, you'll grow to love your spouse as Christ loved the church, and your marriage will thrive.

I'm still learning this principle and have to die to myself many times daily. Since you're reading this book, I assume you're still learning also. Enjoy and learn from temporary challenging life seasons that prepare you for your permanent stay-at-home-man lifestyle, and ultimately, the final reward for every believer in Jesus Christ—eternity with our Lord. Rest assured that as the Bible promises, God knows all and has a good and perfect plan for your life.

Janet and I thank you for caring enough for your spouse, and your relationship, to pick up this book and embrace it. As Jesus taught us, let your light shine and share *Dear God, He's Home!* with someone else going through a season of challenge with her stay-at-home man.

Blessings during this season of your life.

Janet's encourager, cheerleader, loving and
devoted stay-at-home man, Dave

SANITY TOOLS

At the end of that time, I, Nebuchadnezzar, raised my eyes toward heaven, and my sanity was restored. Then I praised the Most High; I honored and glorified him who lives forever. . . . At the same time that my sanity was restored, my honor and splendor were returned to me for the glory of my kingdom. —DANIEL 4:34, 36

RESEARCH NOTES

Source ⸻

Notes ⸻

⸻

⸻

⸻

⸻

⸻

⸻

⸻

Source ⸻

Notes ⸻

⸻

⸻

⸻

⸻

⸻

⸻

⸻

⸻

BOOKS AND RESOURCES

6 Secrets to a Lasting Love by Gary and Barb Rosberg

Face-to-Face with Euodia and Syntyche: From Conflict to Community by Janet Thompson

Face-to-Face with Priscilla and Aquila: Balancing Life and Ministry by Janet Thompson

Face-to-Face with Sarah, Rachel, and Hannah: Pleading with God by Janet Thompson

Honey, I'm Home for Good! by Mary Ann Cook

How to Get Your Husband to Listen to You by Nancy Cobb and Connie Grigsby

Jesus Calling by Sarah Young

JOY-spirations for Caregivers by Annetta Dellinger and Karen Boerger

Plan B by Pete Wilson

Retired with Husband by Mary Louse Floyd (not Christian-based, but has good tips)

The Golden Years Ain't for Wimps by Karen O'Connor (karenoconnor.com)

Too Much Togetherness: Surviving Retirement as a Couple by Miriam Goodman

We All Married Idiots by Elaine W. Miller

We're Finally Alone—Now What Do We Do? by Greg Johnson

When a Woman Inspires Her Husband by Cindi McMenamin

Why Can't HE Be More Like ME? by Poppy Smith

SPECIFIC FOR MILITARY

Called to Serve and *Honored to Serve* by Lt. Col. Tony Monetti and Penny Monetti

Faith Deployed by Jocelyn Green

Faith Deployed . . . Again by Jocelyn Green (faithdeployed.com)

Hope for the Home Front by Marshéle Carter Waddell

Welcome Home Military Marriage Conference: Discover the Love of Your Life All Over Again. Two-disc DVD set by Gary and Barbara Rosberg

When War Comes Home by Chris and Rahnella Adsit and Marshéle Carter Waddell

The VA offers marriage retreats for returning vets: va.gov/health/NewsFeatures/20120223a.asp

ARTICLES BY JOCELYN GREEN:

"Renegotiating Leadership After Deployment," focusonthefamily.com/marriage/military_marriage/the-chain-of-command-in-marriage/renegotiating-the-lead-after-deployment.aspx

"Who's In Charge Here?" focusonthefamily.com/marriage/military_marriage/the-chain-of-command-in-marriage/whos-in-charge-here.aspx

"Solo Duty," focusonthefamily.com/marriage/military_marriage/the-chain-of-command-in-marriage/solo-duty.aspx

"Order in the Home," focusonthefamily.com/marriage/military_marriage/the-chain-of-command-in-marriage/order-in-the-home.aspx

"The Chain of Command in Marriage," focusonthefamily.com/marriage/military_marriage/the-chain-of-command-in-marriage.aspx

MAKING DECISIONS AND DEVELOPING A PLAN

Decisions and options accompany every transition. Prayerfully developing a plan in advance and establishing parameters you both agree on will alleviate anxiety and pressure later. Use the following questions to help formulate your plan. Pray and discuss your answers together:

- What are you both willing to sacrifice?
- What is your main goal?
- What are the financial ramifications?
- What is your budget?
- What are your resources?
- What are your options and which do you prefer?
- What timeframe before considering other options?
- What will be the division of responsibilities?
- What needs to change to maintain a peaceful home?
- What hobbies could you develop together and separately?
- What obstacles can you foresee?
- What other things to consider?

Your Plan:

PEACEKEEPING WORK SHEET

PEACEKEEPING WORK SHEET FOR DECISION ABOUT:

_____

Facts from Personal Experience

_____

_____

_____

Facts from Research

_____

_____

_____

Facts from Consultations

_____

_____

_____

Input from Respected Family/Friends/Mentors

_____

_____

_____

Financial and Time Ramifications

_____

_____

_____

Time with God in Prayer and Reading the Bible

_____

_____

_____

Discussion Together of Thoughts, Opinions, and Desires

_____

_____

_____

Our Peace-Filled Decision Is:

_____

_____

SIGNS OF DEPRESSION

List of Major Depression Symptoms Compiled by Mayo Clinic (mayoclinic
.com/health/depression/DS00175/DSECTION=symptoms)

❑ Feelings of sadness or unhappiness
❑ Irritability or frustration, even over small matters
❑ Loss of interest or pleasure in normal activities
❑ Reduced sex drive
❑ Insomnia or excessive sleeping
❑ Changes in appetite—decreased appetite and weight loss, but can also cause increased food cravings and weight gain
❑ Agitation or restlessness—pacing, hand-wringing or an inability to sit still
❑ Slowed thinking, speaking, or body movements
❑ Indecisiveness, distractibility, and decreased concentration
❑ Fatigue, tiredness, and loss of energy—even small tasks seem to require a lot of effort
❑ Feelings of worthlessness or guilt, fixating on past failures or blaming yourself when things aren't going right
❑ Trouble thinking, concentrating, making decisions, and remembering
❑ Frequent thoughts of death, dying, or suicide
❑ Crying spells for no apparent reason
❑ Unexplained physical problems, such as back pain or headaches
❑ For some, symptoms are so severe it's obvious something isn't right. Others feel generally miserable or unhappy without really knowing why.
❑ Depression affects each person in different ways, so depression symptoms vary from person to person. Inherited traits, age, gender, and cultural background all play a role in how depression may affect you.

THE STEPS OF GRIEF

Adapted from *Dear God, They Say It's Cancer* by Janet Thompson

> *You will grieve, but your grief will suddenly turn to wonderful joy when you see me again.* — JOHN 16:20 (NLT)

❑ *Shock* is the first reaction. The punch or sinking sensation in the pit of your stomach—dizzying, nauseating, room spinning, unbelievable!
❑ *Denial* is a survival reaction until you get your bearings. "This can't be happening to me." You hold on to the possibility it's all a mistake and try ignoring it.
❑ *Acknowledgment* replaces denial. Now you must face it head-on, and it hurts so bad and makes you so mad!

❑ *Anger* often is intense. Maybe you aren't angered easily, but now you are *angry*—angry with yourself, genetics, your circumstances, and maybe God.

❑ *Acceptance* results from anger because you can't be angry at something you haven't accepted.

❑ *Sadness* seeps in as the dust settles on anger and the emotional and physical pain of acceptance engulfs you.

❑ *Depression* is the deepest form of sadness and can become debilitating and dangerous if you don't take steps to move through it.

❑ *Joy* can be the aftermath of healthy grieving, with prayer, support, counsel, and time.

7 STEPS TO BIBLICALLY RESOLVING CONFLICT

Adapted from *Face-to-Face with Euodia and Syntyche: From Conflict to Community* by Janet Thompson

Pray together before going through these steps. Ask your husband if he will also use them when he has an issue with you. Read each step and look up the supporting Scriptures.

1. *Take the initiative to resolve the conflict* (Matthew 5:23–24; 18:15–17).

   The moment you sense a problem in your relationship, take the first step toward righting it—even if you think the other person was wrong and you've done nothing to provoke him. If possible, approach him face-to-face. Letters, email, texting, or phone calls seldom resolve conflict because we can't read each other's face, eyes, or body language. If face-to-face isn't feasible, use the phone or Skype so you can proceed with the following steps.

2. *Focus on goals bigger than your personal differences* (Ephesians 4:3; Philippians 3:12–14). Before starting a discussion, establish that the relationship is more important than any disagreement.

3. *Listen attentively as the other person tells how he or she sees the situation* (Proverbs 18:13; 29:20).

   Let him speak first while you *listen* with your heart, eyes, and ears without becoming defensive or angry. Empathize as you hear the hurt in his voice. Don't interrupt. Let him complete his story.

4. *Validate the person's feelings without minimizing his concerns* (James 1:19–20). Acknowledge his points, without arguing or challenging. Then ask if he'll listen to you.

5. *Tell your story* (Proverbs 18:17).

   Indicate you understand how he may have *perceived* the situation in a different way than you meant it. Avoid assigning blame. It's OK to let him know how the situation hurt your feelings.

6. *Apologize and ask forgiveness for your part in the disagreement* (Colossians 3:13; 1 John 1:9–10).

Don't expect him to say he's sorry or to ask for forgiveness. Forgive with no hidden agenda or expectations.

7. *Discuss how to avoid future conflict* (Proverbs 17:14).

Set ground rules for the relationship going forward. Close with prayer.

TIPS FOR PRAYING AS A COUPLE

Excerpts from *Praying for Your Prodigal Daughter* by Janet Thompson

If you prayed as much as you worried, you wouldn't have as much to worry about!

If you haven't experienced praying as a couple, try these suggestions. Praying together might seem awkward at first, but you'll feel an amazing peace as you pray for each other and the issues facing your marriage.

• Make praying together a priority in your day.

• Find a place to pray without interruption.

• Determine a time that fits both your schedules and put it on your calendars.

• If you choose morning, make it a pleasant time over a cup of coffee or tea.

• If you choose evening, pray before you get into bed, because both of you probably will be exhausted at the end of the day and it'll be hard to stay awake.

• Take turns praying. If one of you is more comfortable than the other praying aloud, have that person start and the other spouse join in or say his or her own prayer. Or do conversational prayer where you each alternate praying, just like talking to each other.

• Start with short prayers until you get used to praying together.

• Write down things you want to remember in prayer. It's OK to pray with your eyes open so you can look at your notes. Hold hands or embrace while you pray.

• Don't be critical of each other's prayers—be encouraging.

• Remember, prayer is just talking to God. You don't have to use big theological terms or sound "spiritual." Just pour out your heart to the only One who can really help.

MORE WORDS OF WISDOM FROM WIVES
WITH A STAY-AT-HOME MAN
Used by permission of Teri Lynne Underwood (terilynneu.com)

- Make each day the best it can be. You don't know how many days you'll have left together. —Alice
- Understand where your husband is at in his life and don't make his retirement or at-home-experience miserable. —Alice
- Don't belittle or put down your husband—build him up. Find out his concerns and needs, don't just focus on your own. —Alice
- Communicate your needs honestly and lovingly. —Joan
- When shopping together, pick a store with a sporting, gardening, or electronic department and let your husband browse or find something for you. —Sue
- What's important to your spouse should also be important to you and what's important to God should be important to both of you! —Janet

10 WAYS TO SPEAK WELL OF YOUR HUSBAND
Used by permission of Teri Lynne Underwood (terilynneu.com)

1. Speak well of him in your prayers. Rather than asking God to change him, spend some time asking God to show you how to pray for him.
2. Speak well of him to yourself. Remind yourself of those things you love about your husband.
3. Speak well of him to your children.
4. Speak well of him to your mother. I know the temptation to "vent" to your mom when he drives you crazy. Resist! You'll move past it . . . she might not. (This applies to everyone in your family as well.)
5. Speak well of him to his family. No matter how close you are to your in-laws, it's never a good idea to vocalize those personal frustrations you have about your husband to them.
6. Speak well of him to your friends. Don't join in the "husband bashing." It's a dangerous path!
7. Speak well of him to other women. You have a great opportunity to model being a supportive wife for those who are watching you. (Use discernment about what you share and with whom.)
8. Speak well of him to his co-workers (or former co-workers) and their wives. Be cautious about sharing personal details with your husband's co-workers but never speak disparagingly about him to those with whom he works.
9. Speak well of him whenever the opportunity presents itself! But may I suggest that you be wise in what and where you share. It's easy to use a Facebook status to express your fondness, but make sure your motivation is truly to bless him and not to draw attention to yourself. After all, if he is a private person, he may not appreciate the public attention.
10. Speak well of him to him. Take time to communicate with your husband your appreciation for who he is and what he does. How do you speak well of your husband?

HUMOROUS RETIREMENT TO-DO LIST* (SAMPLE)

	SUN	MON	TUES	WED	THURS	FRI	SAT
Make breakfast in bed for your wife							
Prepare coffee for your wife							
Feed the dogs							
Pet the cats							
Make the bed							
Load dishwasher (this means rinsing the dishes)							
Unload dishwasher							
Wipe off countertops							
Pretreat spots on front of your shirts							
Wash stovetop							
Wash a few windows							
Clean the kitchen sink							
Sharpen knives							
Clean the garage							
Take a hike							
Read a book							
Check in with the guys to see if anybody has any ideas for something to do							
Read another book							
Call your dad							
Take the dogs for a walk							
Check on the cats							
See if anybody has come up with anything to do							
Vacuum the floors							
Call them one more time!							
Clean up the garage (again)							
Torment the dogs							
Irritate the cats							
Call them again!							

Note: *Always wear glasses when performing any required duties.*
Created by Carol Lynde, wife of a retired Army Lieutenant Colonel

I AM SO HAPPY BECAUSE . . .

I'm so glad to have this stay-at-home man around to discuss things with and defer decisions to. It sure takes the responsibility off of me.

— NANCY

As I found things to be thankful and appreciative for during Richard's unemployment, against all odds, I began to feel rich. — CHAR

Who am I, O Lord God, and what is my family, that you have brought me this far? — 1 CHRONICLES 17:16

Things to Be Grateful for

_____

_____

_____

_____

_____

_____

_____

_____

_____

_____

_____

_____

_____

_____

_____

_____

_____

_____

_____

_____

I Have Many Blessings

_____

_____

_____

_____

_____

_____

_____

_____

_____

_____

_____

_____

_____

_____

_____

_____

_____

_____

_____

_____

PRAYER AND PRAISE JOURNAL

I began to track improvements in our situation while claiming the promises of Psalm 1:2–3 (paraphrased): *"I delight in the Lord and meditate on his law day and night. I will be like a tree, growing by a stream of water which produces refreshing seasonal fruit. My leaves will never wither, and whatever I do will prosper."* — CHAR

Prayer

Praise

SMALL-GROUP GUIDE

You can easily adapt *Dear God, He's Home!* to a small support group for wives or couples. I suggest members read a chapter between meetings and then get together to discuss the "For Discussion" section at the end of each chapter. Below, I have provided a sample format for the group meetings and an opening icebreaker for each chapter.

You might have a focus group of members all sharing the same reason for the husband being home, or mix it up and have a diversified group. Just as you've found in this book, the reasons for having a stay-at-home man may differ, but the issues are often similar and the solutions—God's Word and God's ways—always apply, regardless of circumstances.

Select a discussion leader or rotate that privilege. The leader keeps the group on track and doesn't let it turn into a gripe or gossip session. The purpose of this group is to share tips and ideas for living cohesively and in harmony with your stay-at-home man in a way that honors God and your marriage.

There will be times of serious discussion, but allow time for laughter too. When I was writing this book and shared snippets with others, my husband noted that everyone, including him, was laughing. He asked me if this was going to be a humorous book. So have fun, but don't minimize a painful or difficult issue a member may be encountering.

SUPPORT GROUP GUIDELINES:

1. Don't share personal information embarrassing to your spouse. In couples' groups, don't tell stories without your spouses' permission.
2. Everything discussed in the group stays in the group.
3. Make sure everyone has an opportunity to share and one person doesn't dominate the time.
4. This isn't a counseling session. It's OK to give tips and suggestions that have worked for you, but don't try to "fix" another person's situation.
5. Prayer requests stay within the group unless given permission to ask others for prayer.

SUGGESTED GROUP FORMAT:

❑ Open in prayer.
❑ Icebreaker
❑ "For Discussion" section at the end of each chapter
❑ Ask each participant to name one or more things he or she gained from this chapter and how they will apply it to their marriage.
❑ General Discussion
❑ Prayer Requests
❑ Fellowship

ICEBREAKERS FOR EACH CHAPTER

CHAPTER 1: HE's HOME!
Icebreaker: Each group member writes on an index card something unusual she/he has done that the others won't know about. Read the cards and everyone try to guess who it is.

CHAPTER 2: PARALYZING SHOCK
Icebreaker: Each member writes on a note card her/his reaction when finding out they were going to have (or be) a stay-at-home man—using no names. Shuffle the cards and have members pick a card that's not their own and try to guess whose card they have.

CHAPTER 3: ADJUSTING PLANS
Icebreaker: Hide two objects in different places in a room. Break the group into two teams and have each team search for one of the objects. Team rules: Teams have to stay together at all times and if they find the other team's object, they are to leave it and not say anything. When one team finds their object first, announce them as the losing team—a game changer. Discuss the plus and minuses of staying in their teams and how it felt to lose when you thought you won.

CHAPTER 4: ESTABLISHING A NEW NORMAL
Icebreaker: Bring a magnet and let each person find something the magnet draws to in the room. Discuss how the diversity of magnetic items relates to the diversity of situations in the stay-at-home man magnet syndrome.

CHAPTER 5: DEALING WITH REACTIONS
Icebreaker: Have each member share a funny and unpleasant reaction—from family or friends—to their stay-at-home man scenario.

CHAPTER 6: GETTING NEEDED SUPPORT
Icebreaker: Have each member describe how she/he derives support outside of this group. Note the variety mentioned.

CHAPTER 7: MAKING IT THROUGH THE BAD DAYS
Icebreaker: Ask if anyone is having a tough time and pray for that person. Don't rush into the discussion until they're ready.

CHAPTER 8: ENJOYING THE GOOD DAYS
Icebreaker: Read the fictitious story of the stay-at-home man at Walmart on page 92. Have a good laugh and then ask if anyone wants to share a humorous stay-at-home man antic.

CHAPTER 9: KNOWING WHO IS IN CONTROL
Icebreaker: Ask each member to come up with a metaphor or simile that best depicts her/his sense of being out of control during this stay-at-home man experience.

CHAPTER 10: GRIEVING THE LOSSES
Icebreaker: Ask each member to mention one loss they've grieved during the stay-at-home man transition. If anyone needs prayer, stop and pray.

CHAPTER 11: DISCOVERING A NEW FOCUS AND PURPOSE
Icebreaker: Write the names of biblical couples on name tags. When each member arrives, put a nametag on her/his back, without saying who it is. Members ask each other questions about the couple on their own name tag to get clues as to who is "on their back."

CHAPTER 12: RELYING ON GOD
Icebreaker: Put out a coin or paper money and point out the inscription "In God We Trust." Ask why they think our forefathers put that on money and what the phrase means in our marriages.

CHAPTER 13: RESTORING THE JOY
Icebreaker: Sing an opening joyful song

CHAPTER 14: ENDING AT THE BEGINNING
Icebreaker: Ask for the most important thing they learned from reading this book.

ABOUT HIS WORK MINISTRIES

About His Work Ministries is Janet Thompson's writing and speaking ministry. Janet is about His work helping women realize the importance and value of relationships and God's call in Titus 2:1–5 to teach and train the next generation through mentoring and sharing life experiences. In 1996, Janet answered God's call to "Feed My sheep" by founding the Woman to Woman Mentoring Ministry at Saddleback Church in Lake Forest, California. Through her authored resources, *Woman to Woman Mentoring: How to Start, Grow, and Maintain a Mentoring Ministry* (LifeWay Press) and "Face-to-Face" Bible study series (New Hope Publishers), Janet has helped churches around the world start Woman to Woman Mentoring in their own churches.

FOR MORE INFORMATION AND TO CONTACT JANET

About His Work Ministries—Conference and retreat speaking, mentoring, and coaching aspiring writers and ministry leaders

Two About His Work—Janet and her daughter Kim's conference and retreat speaking ministry

Email: info@womantowomanmentoring.com • facebook.com/janetthompson .authorspeaker • womantowomanmentoring.com • twitter.com/ ThompsonDearGod • pinterest.com/thompsonjanet

Please share with Janet how this book has enriched your marriage to your stay-at-home man.

Your Next Read . . .

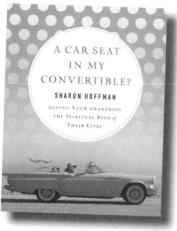
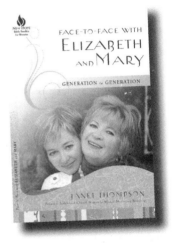

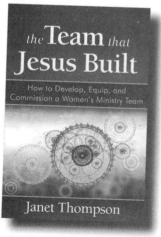

Get more out of your reading experience with free book-club guides, small-group study guides, and more at NewHopeDigital.com

---

New Hope® Publishers is a division of WMU®, an international organization that challenges Christian believers to understand and be radically involved in God's mission. For more information about WMU, go to wmu.com. More information about New Hope books may be found at NewHopeDigital.com. New Hope books may be purchased at your local bookstore.

Use the QR reader on your
smartphone to visit us online at
NewHopeDigital.com

If you've been blessed by this book, we would like to hear your story. The publisher and author welcome your comments and suggestions at: newhopereader@wmu.org.